EVERYTHING YOU NEED TO KNOW FOR

COACHING
RUGBY

EVERYTHING YOU NEED TO KNOW FOR

COACHING RUGBY

INCLUDING MORE THAN 100 DRILLS & GAMES
FOR COACHING ALL THE BASICS

Credits, acknowledgements and legal notices

First published in PDF and Spiral Bound format 2007 by Rugby Coach Weekly

www.rugbycoachweekly.co.uk

Paperback edition published June 2015

ISBN: 978-1-910338-43-8

The right of Dan Cottrell to be identified as the author of this work has been asserted by him in accordance with the Copyright, Designs and Patents Act 1988.

Green Star Media Ltd. Company No: 3008779. VAT Registration No: 668031727. Registered under the Data Protection Act 1998. No: Z5287130

Credits
Author: Dan Cottrell
Contributor: Paul Tyler
Editor: Toby Curthoys
Cover design: Matt Boulton
Cover photograph: Luke Ehrlanderr
Layout design: Natalie Schmidt, Julie Lifton
Illustrations: Mike Ronald
Production: Matt Boulton
Marketing: Kevin Barrow, Hayley Booth
Customer services: Duncan Heard, Ben Hodges
Publisher: Andrew Griffiths

The author would like to thank Warren Robilliard, Coach Education Manager for the Australian Rugby Union (ARU) and John Schropfer, Regional Community Manager for the Welsh Rugby Union (WRU) for their invaluable help and advice in the production of this publication.

Grateful thanks to London Irish RFC for permission to use the cover image.

Green Star Media Ltd
Meadow View, Tannery Lane, Bramley, Guildford, Surrey GU5 0AB
T: +44 (0)1483 892894   Email: customerservices@greenstarmedia.net

Contents

Foreword to the second edition

By Sir Clive Woodward

The business of coaching the game of rugby union has come a long way since I started playing and coaching. Advances in understanding about fitness and nutrition have transformed the professional game and the use of technology and modern coaching techniques continue to make an impact.

At grassroots level, the picture is rather different. Thousands of amateur mums and dads support community rugby, managing and coaching in their spare time, fitting in a coaching course if they can, picking up ideas and support where it is available.

When they start coaching rugby, even if they have perhaps played, there is much to learn: dealing with the fundamental challenges of coaching on top of understanding the laws and techniques of what is a complex and technical game.

This is where independent coaching resources like *Coaching Rugby* come in. This commendable manual, which has stood the test of time, addresses in detail the questions of what to coach and, most importantly, how to coach.

Coaching Rugby contains guidance for all the basics. Previously only available online, it is now available to a wider audience in paperback format in bookstores.

In this World Cup year, it represents a timely opportunity for the next generation of coaches coming through to invest in their own learning and development and enhance our much-loved game.

Sir Clive Woodward was coach of the England rugby team from 1997 to 2004, managing them to victory in the 2003 Rugby World Cup. He is also a Team GB Ambassador and the founding partner of Captured, an online knowledge capturing tool.

Foreword to the first edition

By John Schropfer

Throughout my rugby union and teaching career, I have always been involved in rugby coaching. In my opinion, coaches underpin rugby, but too often their work is taken for granted.

Like many of you, I started to coach because somebody needed to… and because I knew I could play a bit and knew something about the game, so I thought that, that "somebody" could be me.

When you start trying to coach children for the first time, however, you quickly realise how much you don't know and how much unconscious technique you take for granted. Coaching children also has an added burden – the rugby future of these youngsters, to a great extent, is in your hands.

If a child's only exposure to rugby is through the training sessions that we, as coaches, run for them, we have a huge responsibility to get it right. These early matches and training sessions will stay with the players for the rest of their lives. But it's simply not enough to get a qualification and then coach.

I am delighted to say that *Coaching Rugby* goes beyond the standard qualifications to describe exactly what needs to be taught in practical terms. It emphasises not just the "how to manage a group of players", but also "how to coach", "what to coach", and "what to observe and analyse" if players are not performing a skill to the correct "outcome".

It is an authoritative source, full of proven training techniques and coaching plans to lead new coaches through the minefield of their first coaching year.

Indeed, I think *Coaching Rugby* provides a significant stepping stone for new coaches who wish to encourage, engage and develop the skills of every young player within their charge. Thus laying the foundations which will enable them to reach their full potential. All the time emphasising having fun playing rugby!

John Schropfer is the National Community Coach Education Manager for the Welsh Rugby Union. He is a former Assistant Welsh National Coach and is a member of the UKCC Rugby Source Group, which develops the rugby coaching courses across England, Scotland and Wales.

How to use this manual

Coaching Rugby is designed to build your players' techniques, skills and understanding of the whole game. It is divided into two parts:

1. The basics of working with young players in a safe and rewarding environment.

2. More than 100 training sessions and game situations for a coach to use with any age group to develop the basic skills of rugby union.

Many of the training sessions included in the Manual take the players' initial skills to the next stages. Additional games, game situations and extensive developments allow the coach to revisit the sessions and reinforce the skills a number of times during the season, whilst ensuring that the training remains fresh and relevant.

It is, in fact, entirely possible for a coach to build a season around the sessions contained in *Coaching Rugby*.

The Manual is primarily aimed at new coaches and coaches who are covering unfamiliar areas, although it also provides an excellent source of ideas for more experienced coaches looking for a fresh approach to their regular sessions. It was written to support those coaches working on or towards their IRB Coaches Level 1 courses and beyond.

All coaches can use the Manual in conjunction with the long term player development formula to support players between the ages of 8 and 16 years old, as identified on pages 17 and 18.

Safety and environment

A safe practice means better outcomes for everyone involved:
- There is less chance of injury.
- Players and coaches are more motivated in a safe environment.
- There wlll be higher retention rates among the players.

Safety first

A good coach always questions the safety aspects of all their coaching interventions. If you can do this BEFORE the session, problems can be foreseen and dealt with.

Risk assessments play an important part in managing the health and safety of your team. With our five key factor "PEACE" of mind guide, risk assessments are not quite as daunting as you might think.

P is for "Players"

Medical history – Do you have the correct up to date medical records for all your players, with easy to find information on allergies and conditions?

If something happens on the pitch side, then the attending medical staff will be keen to know crucial details like blood type or current medication. Keep a sheet with you at all times during training, matches, and whilst travelling with your players.

Current fitness – Do not force any player to play. You need to be wary of the player who tries to play when they are carrying an injury. Be careful of the "fun" game or practice situation: for instance, games that become overly boisterous or aggressive.

Players' clothing and equipment – Always start before training or a match with a quick check of your players' outfits, including a careful look for jewellery (like wristwatches, rings and earrings). Though rugby studs are checked before the start of every match, make sure you make regular checks in training too.

E is for "Equipment"

Rugby uses a range of extra equipment to train: various types of contact bags, scrum machines, elastic ropes, sledges, poles, ladders and hurdles. Before training, a routine check can ensure they pose no danger to the users. Check for sharp edges or abrasive materials.

Scrum machines need special attention as outlined in the manufacturers' instructions. The main problems can occur from loose pads or worn out apparatus.

Equipment safety checklist:
- Scrum machines.
- Tackle bags and ruck pads.
- Post protectors.
- Corner flags.
- Ladders.
- Hurdles.
- Weighted balls.
- Personal equipment (e.g. mouthguards, headgear).

A is for "Area"

Training and playing need appropriate surfaces. A walk through the area before the activity will highlight the dangers, such as uneven ground, debris and areas which are too hard or too soft. It is worth noting the sides of the playing area need monitoring as well. Fencing, walls and even spectators can cause a risk to normal play.

You are aware that weather conditions cause problems, but it can be difficult to assess the level of risk involved. Frozen grounds are particularly problematic since they are "unexpected" hard ground conditions. Here is a simple test to see they are fit to play on. Punch the ground with your fist. If it hurts, then imagine what contact with the ground in the same way might do to one of your players' heads.

C is for "Crucial information"

There should be clear signage at the ground and in the club house. This is to both aid visitors and enable a successful evacuation if required. All matters to do with health and safety at the ground should be clearly displayed for all players, spectators, officials and staff.

E is for "Emergency points"

It is a priority that any rugby training activity takes place where:

- There is access for emergency vehicles.
- A working telephone is available, with emergency numbers easily accessible. In fact, it may be a requirement of your or your club's insurance that you carry a working, adequately charged mobile phone with you at all times during training, matches, and whilst travelling.

How often should I do a risk assessment?

A risk assessment should be carried out for every training or playing event. It is not a long process and if you follow the PEACE of mind guide, then you should have covered the key areas.

The longer term implications need to be considered at least once a season, with checks made on major club and team policies. The major unions offer specific training courses and guidance on how to improve their rugby specific skills in these areas.

Risk assessment terms

Hazard – Anything that has the potential to cause harm. Do you have measures in place to reduce the chances of someone being harmed by the hazard? For instance, do you carry out regular safety checks?

Risk factor – The likelihood of something happening. High risk (could occur quite easily), medium risk (could occur sometimes), low risk (unlikely, but possible).

Can you control the risk factors or react appropriately? For instance, could there be more medical education for you and your coaches?

Ethical and legal coaching

Ethical coaching means coaching in a manner which is, in your opinion, morally right. This view can change from coach to coach. However, all the major unions have similar guidelines for ethical coaching.

Legal matters

You must coach within the laws of the land. You must pay attention to health and safety, violent and abusing conduct, and discriminatory behaviour.

From the English RFU

Ethics – Creating a positive environment with good sporting attitudes.

Equity/social inclusion – Welcoming people from all backgrounds to the game.

The principles of safety, equity, child protection, enjoyment, and law need to be properly established.

Legal responsibilities and children

Child protection is an important legal and moral concern for coaches. You need to protect your players from child abuse and, in turn, protect yourself from potential accusations of wrongful behaviour.

All the major unions run courses to make coaches aware of the potential signs of abuse. Things to be aware of include neglect, emotional abuse, sexual abuse and physical abuse. Remember that physical abuse can be present in children who are being physically pushed too hard in terms of their rugby – be on the look out for over training. Also watch out for the use of drugs to enhance performance.

If a child approaches you with information, follow these procedures rigidly:

1) Listen without prejudice.
2) Tell the child they were right to tell you.
3) Tell the child that you are going to tell someone else, no matter what they say to the contrary, then do it!
4) Make a written note of everything that was said and your action as a response to the child's allegation.
5) Immediately inform your club's child welfare office or approach your rugby union about the allegation.

If you suspect abuse, you should:

1) Share your concerns with your club's or union's child welfare officer to decide on the best procedure. Then act on it.
2) Only approach the parents for further information if you think it will not put the child at risk.

Act professionally:

1) Don't coach one-on-one unless there is another adult present.
2) Never give out your personal contact details.

The coach's role and the referee

Respect the referee. It sends out the right messages to your and other players, and maintains a calm atmosphere for learning and development.

From New Zealand's "Rugby Smart"

"One of the great things rugby teaches people is discipline. It's one of the qualities a coach can instil in players. Don't tolerate foul play – particularly anything like any dangerous tackles or thuggery. Referee abuse is unacceptable at any level of the sport."

Fair play

Coach your players to respect their opponents and the laws. Maintain your dignity whether you are winning or losing, because the sport is more important than one game.

Coaching children

Having fun is fundamental to coaching. You create the circumstances in which your players can enjoy themselves. The environment therefore should be:

- **Safe.**
- **Non threatening.**
- **Encouraging mutual respect between your players.**

"FUN" principles

- **F** is for **"Fun"** – Engagement and learning come from enjoyable and worthwhile experiences. Keep your players coming back week in, week out with fun sessions as well as by looking after technique.

- **U** is for **"Understanding"** – Children are not little adults. You need to take into account growth spurts, hormonal changes and mental maturity.

- **N** is for **"Nurturing"** – Coaching children is a journey. Winning is only one of the many positive experiences involved. Coaching only to win will lose you players in the long run. Instead, watch each individual grow over the years, not the team over a season.

Play

Whilst practising in a competitive environment is essential, playing games to enhance skills is vital. (The chapter about Long Term Player Development on page 13 outlines the suggested ratio of play to coaching to games.)

Through playing, children will learn many of the principles of rugby without having to resort to lots of drills. Try devising games that challenge skill levels.

Winning versus development

Research shows that the majority of children would prefer to play in a losing team, than not play but be in the squad of a winning team. Competition has its place, but should be seen as a benchmark not as a goal.

Use goals other than winning to set the standards for your team. For example:

1) An improvement in results.
2) Conceding fewer points than last time.

Similarly, set individual targets, such as tackles completed, successful passes made.

These targets and goals should be challenging but achievable. All players, especially children, need to see their skills improve and understand that their hard work in practice is paying off.

Winning and motivation

Motivation means the desire to achieve a goal. The more motivated you are, the more you will try to achieve that goal.

There are a range of reasons why children play rugby, and winning is not always the priority. It depends on the individual. You need to take this into account when you try to motivate your players individually and as a team.

Coaching children rugby union

Friendship, individual successes, recognition and belonging can play an important part in what motivates each player.

Treating children as rugby players

The physical presence and mental maturity of each child must be taken into account at all times.

Since children grow at different rates, they may be a big difference in your players' size over a year group. Match sizes carefully. There is little to gain from a big mismatch. The large player can impose themselves physically and the smaller player will need to rely on guts and determination. This will be to the detriment of technical expertise.

Children can learn quickly. They are not, however, necessarily good at assimilating information in an ordered fashion. Telling a player something one week will not mean it is remembered for next week. Concentration levels will improve over time, but don't be surprised if a player's mind wanders during a session.

Session rules

Coaching children in sessions can be problematic. Here are a few simple rules to help make training easier:

1) **The length of the session** – No longer than two of their normal school lesson times and with a break in the middle.

2) **Imbue good habits at all times** – Correct bad practice and technique immediately.

3) **Don't push your players too hard** – Leave them wanting more, not crawling off the training ground.

4) **Don't do practices that are dangerous** –

Be extra vigilant when doing anything involving contact.

Your legacy

The best legacy to have as a coach is when a young player continues to play rugby after leaving your team and then for the rest of their playing career.

You can help create this situation by:

1) Giving your players every opportunity to play rugby.

2) Rotating playing positions to help your players develop "all round" skills and knowledge.

3) Letting your players play as many other sports as possible. It will add to their game sense, physical attributes and keep them fresh.

Best practice communication with children

1) **Positive statements** – Avoid sarcasm. Criticism should involve tips for improvement.

2) **Use short term goals as targets** – They're easier to understand and results can be seen sooner. This will motivate children further.

3) **Repetition and recap** – Make your players feedback as well.

4) **Communicate without pressure** – Fear of giving a wrong answer can be as upsetting as giving the wrong answer. It holds back players.

5) **Inclusive environment** – Anyone should feel they can be part of the communication process.

6) **Bad language** – This is never appropriate with children of any age.

7) **Short sentences** – Raise only a few points and move on.

Coaching through questioning

Research* shows that learning comes from self discovery. This means players realise how to solve problems and react to situations by finding their own solutions. Coaches should try to reduce the amount of time they spend "telling" the players what to do. Instead, through questioning, they should look to empower their players.

To aid good learning the coach needs to communicate well verbally.

Verbal communication is the use of words to convey a message. The choice of words is often not as important as the way they are told. Remember:

- Don't use jargon.
- Don't use sarcasm.
- Promote positive comments.
- Criticism should be backed up with a way forward.

In giving verbal communication:

- Keep sentences short.
- Don't make too many points.
- Summarise at the end – some players may not have understood the first time around.

Verbal communication and questioning

Asking questions is useful because:

- It gains the attention of the players.
- The coach learns what the players already know.
- It involves the players in the learning process.
- It allows the players to express their opinions.
- It helps the coach check for understanding.

Asking the best questions

- Use open questions – questions that cannot be answered with just "yes" or "no". Start questions with words, like "what", "how" or "where".
- Don't use "why", because it can be construed as negative.
- Wait for the answer, don't hurry the player.
- When listening to the answer, listen, don't anticipate the answer. Try not to rephrase the answer once given.

Coaching through questioning

When to "tell" and when to "question"

Tell:

- You have a short period of time to get your point across.
- Specific instructions are needed. For instance, health and safety issues or laws of the game.
- A larger group makes question and answer sessions unwieldy.

Question:

- To check your players' understanding.
- To gain feedback.
- To improve your players' learning.

Dealing with the "wrong" answer, some positive coaching responses

- "That might not work in this situation. In what situation could it be used?"
- "Thank you for your answer, I liked your imaginative response. Have you thought how that might be used in this situation?"
- "That's an unusual idea. How can you see that working here?"

* For example: Wixson, K.K. "Questions About a Test: What you Ask About Is What Children Learn." Reading Teacher 37(1983): 287-93.

Dealing with the "wrong" answer, some "DON'TS"

- Don't use words like "but" or "however".
- Don't be afraid to identify the faults in the answer. The player needs to feel valued and know whether his contribution works or is significant.

BUT do rephrase the question to clarify it, or point out a potential opening for the given answer to have some value.

An example coach asking a player questions:

Q: Where was the space?
A: Right in front of us.

Q: Perhaps there was some space there. Have you considered where you might find more space, because the defence looks good here?
A: Wider out?

Q: Good, how could you improve your decision from the ruck?
A: I might have passed earlier.

Q. What would you have done next?
A: Passed it and then followed...

Q: Meaning you could have...? (wait for the answer)
A: Got the ball back.

Long term player development

A child's ability to learn changes as they grow up. It is important that we recognise these developments to improve our own delivery as well as the child's long term development in the sport.

Long term athlete development models, typically like the one proposed by Dr Istvan Bayli, have been adopted by the UK's Home Unions as a template to help understand how to deliver their rugby coaching.

Typically, they split the stages of development based on the approximate ages of the children. It is worth noting that chronological age is not a good indicator of physical or mental maturity between the ages of 10 and 16. Just line up your team to see this. Some children will be more advanced than others between these ages. Notably, girls tend to develop sooner than boys.

Missing a stage in a player's development can mean losing the player to injury, discontent or other pursuits. Players also may not develop as fully as they could and/or become long term injured.

Maintaining the balance between competition and training, plus looking at long term goals, will help ensure players don't reach a plateau in their development because they have missed out on the crucial training phases.

In the Manual we focus on two key stages: "Learning to train" and "Training to train".

The ABCS and the five Ss

A rugby player develops as an athlete by first concentrating on improving their ABCS - that is, agility, balance, co-ordination and speed. As they develop further as rugby players as well as athletes, then a coach should spend more time on the five Ss – that is, speed (again), stamina, strength, skill, and suppleness. The following is a more detailed explanation of these terms:

A – Agility: How quickly a player can start, stop and move their body in different directions.

B – Balance: When a player is in position to move themselves or the ball in any direction they want, without falling over.

C – Co-ordination: The ability to combine the senses to perform acts such as catching and passing the ball.

S – Speed: How quickly the player moves across the ground.

Long term athlete development

FUNdamental stage	Learning to train stage	Training to train stage	Training to compete	Training to win
Males 6-9 Females 6-8	Males 9-12 Females 8-11	Males 12-16 Females 11-15	Males 16-18 Females 15-17	Males 18+ Females 17+

Long term player development

S – Stamina: How long a player can continue to perform at a certain level.

S – Strength: The amount of force that can be exerted by a player.

S – Skill: The use of techniques under pressure.

S – Suppleness: The flexibility of the player's body, allowing greater speed, co-ordination, skill and prevention of injury.

The chart on the following pages bring together the elements discussed so far. It balances the child's age and the long term athlete development stage, with the suggested training regime and level of competition.

Summary

1) Maintain a long term training goal for young players.

2) Don't move to position specific training for individuals until they have passed their growth spurts.

3) Concentrate on core skills over tactical appreciation in the early stages.

4) Balance the competition to training ratio based on the children's ages.

5) Focus on the athletic ability of the player, known as the ABCS – agility, balance, coordination and speed. Then move to the full five Ss – speed, stamina, strength, skill and suppleness.

Ages	LTAD Model Stage	Training	Competition
Males: 6-9 Females: 6-8	FUNdamental stage	Concentrate on movement skills, agility, balance, coordination and speed (ABCS). Includes catching. Only body weight strength training (for example press-ups).	Play lots of different sports, not just rugby. Play lots of fun games. Train and play no more than twice a week.
Males: 9-12 Females: 8-11	Learning to train stage	Improve ABCS. Work on sports skills (rugby related core skills of kicking, handling, tackling, contact, evasion). Improve flexibility. Start to use games and relays to improve endurance. Only body weight strength training (for example, press-ups).	70:30 ratio training to playing competitive matches.
Males: 12-16 Females: 11-15	Training to train stage	"Building the engine" and consolidating the core skills. Flexibility key with the growth surge. Once players have passed their major growth spurt, work on endurance. Concentrate on training for long term goals, not short term "winning".	60:40 ratio of training to playing competitive matches. Coaches need to maintain this balance. It's important to train techniques and put them into practice.
Males: 16-18 Females: 15-17	Training to compete stage	Move players to specific positions. Develop more specific fitness activities depending on the position (for instance, sprinting for wings, weights for props).	50:50 ratio of training to playing competitive matches. More time to be spent on tactical skills.
Males: 18+ Females: 17+	Training to win stage	Maximising fitness, individual and position specific skills.	25:75 ratio of training to playing competitive matches. The competition percentage to include competition specific training activities.

How to use the coaching sessions

Timings

Each session should take you less than five minutes to read and set up. You are then ready to communicate the objectives of the session to your players. The timings are for a 20 minute session, but it can be expanded to meet your needs. It's your call. As a rule of thumb, 10 minutes is enough time for a well executed first drill, development and feedback. Any shorter and you have not explored the full skill range or asked enough questions of the players. Longer is fine as long as you feel the session is developing. The game elements add another 10 minutes.

Number of players

Normally you need a minimum of six players to complete a session, though each can easily be expanded to meet your needs. With more players you can have a number of sessions working at the same time.

Equipment

The equipment used is simple. A set of cones, trainers or tops as markers and a few balls. Add in tackle bags, suits and rucking pads where you feel you need them.

Training area

The smaller the area the more intense the training. Smaller players also need a smaller area. The session will seldom need more than a 20 metre square for initial drills, though some may need more, but the size of the training area is for you to decide.

The standard and age groups

The sessions are based on core rugby skills. They challenge any standard because a player can always perform the core skills better. The "development" ideas can be used to differentiate between the different standards of your players. The "think about" section can challenge the more advanced. The "game related situations" can change the contact situations the teams face.

The session

What you tell your players the session is about:

This is the introduction and outlines the objectives of the session. Just read this out. The players then have an objective. Return to this at the end of the session to see if you have achieved your objectives.

What you tell your players to do:

This is how you want your players to achieve the objectives. You can tell the players about these straight away, or you can tease it out of them as the session goes on.

What you get your players to do:

This shows you how the session is going to work. Depending on what is going to be achieved, it sets out what actions the players are going to take.

There are no exact measurements, or complicated patterns – the approach is "simple, stupid, successful". "Slow motion" the first few patterns – get the drill right and the skill right first before speeding up.

Use the "What to call out" prompts to keep the players focused. Use the "What to look for" prompts to keep your eye on why the players might be failing.

Developing the session

No session is worth doing unless there is some form of progression. Normally there will be an increase in pressure, say by adding more defenders, or by restricting the time available. Other areas for you to think about are: Where do I stand as coach? Do I throw the ball into the box?

A game situation

All the elements of the session are geared to the game. This section puts the session one step away from a full game, with attack, defence and a goal line.

Coach's notes

What to call out

Have the words handy because, apart from the usual words of encouragement, it is good to call out the key factors to players. Of course you can hold some of these "calls" back and ask the players to identify how they can improve.

What to look for

You need to keep your eyes open for "best practice". This section helps you identify quickly where players might go wrong so you can quickly put them right.

What to think about

Here you have the chance to challenge the players and situation, either by using feedback or just asking yourself the questions. It is a little more advanced and might not be appropriate for your players.

Tackling

Tackling preparation

The session

What you tell your players the session is about:

1 Understanding the tackle law – a tackle occurs when the ball carrier is held by one or more opponents and is brought to ground.
2 How to fall safely, both as a tackler and tackled player.

What you tell your players to do:

1 Use your knees, hips and shoulders to impact on the ground, not the arms.
2 Progress slowly, increasing the level of contact.
3 Remember that the ball carrier needs to know how to fall as much as the tackler needs to know how to tackle.

What you get your players to do:

1 Use contact warm up drills.
   ■ Slowly increase the level of intensity.

■ Make sure every player practises with a ball held in both hands.
■ Make sure all players fall to the ground correctly – with no hands out to break the fall.

Example contact warm up drills are:
■ Forward rolls.
■ Parachute falls.
■ Wrestling.

Coach's notes

 What to call out

"Chin off your chest"
"Impact with your shoulder first"
"Tackle with your eyes open"
"Wrap your arms around the ball carrier to form a 'ring of steel' "

"Ball carrier: hold onto the ball with both hands"

 What to look for

The position of the head in contact. In a side on tackle, the head should be tucked behind the ball carrier – "cheek to cheek" or "what smells to what smells". In a front on tackle, the head should be at the side of the body. Loose arms after contact. Most of the "pain" of tackling happens after the impact if the tackler lets go. Emphasise the "ring of steel".

What to think about

What are the types of tackling you should be coaching your players? Passive and aggressive tackles: passive tackles are ones where the tackler uses the body weight and momentum of the tackled player to bring them to the ground, such as front on and rear tackles. Aggressive tackles are where the tackler pushes the tackled player in another direction, such as side on tackles.

Tackling

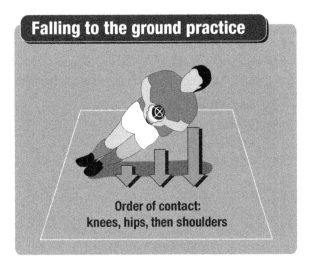

Falling to the ground practice

Order of contact:
knees, hips, then shoulders

2 Practise falling to the ground. The order of
   contact with the ground is:
   i   Knees.
   ii Hips.
   iii Shoulders.

3 The static tackle – a practice involving the middle
   and end sections of a full tackle. One player puts
   one foot in front of the other (heel to toes) whilst
   holding the ball in two hands. Another player is
   then shown the ideal tackling position and grip.
   He takes up this position. The tackle for this
   advanced position is made, ideally onto a mat or
   pad. Check that both players have fallen properly.

Simple tackling

The session

What you tell your players the session is about:

1 Tackling for the first time.
2 Gaining the confidence to make strong tackles on a moving player.

What you tell your players to do:

1 Use your shoulders and then arms to bring a ball carrier to the ground.
2 Concentrate on technique first.

What you get your players to do:

Have one player as a ball carrier and one as the tackler. The tackler will be positioned at right angles to the direction that the ball carrier is facing. Progress the tackles as follows:

Simple tackling

Coach's notes

 What to call out

"Keep your eyes open and your chin off your chest"
"Aim at the ball carrier's thigh"
"Hold on tight to the ball carrier"
"Get your head into the side of the ball carrier"

 What to look for

The tackler's head not pressed against the body of the ball carrier. This probably means the grip is too loose. The tackler may fall away from the tackle, which is unsafe.

The tackled player putting their arm out to their break fall – may need to practise falling techniques (knees, hips, shoulders).

The ball carrier not carrying the ball in two hands at all times.

 What to think about

The type of ground being used. Can you find a soft patch? A crash mat
is useful for hard ground. Are players following through with the tackle and then getting up? Remember the game does not stop with a tackle.

Tackling

1 The ball carrier on their haunches, with the tackler kneeling on their haunches.
2 The ball carrier stands still, with one foot directly in front of the other, heel to toe.
3 The ball carrier walking heel to toe.
4 The ball carrier jogging along a line, each foot touching the line.

Developing the session

The training session can be developed as follows.
1 Change the shoulder that the tackler uses.
2 The tackler has to complete the tackle, by getting to their feet quickly to play the ball.
3 The ball carrier looks to place the ball correctly or pass in the tackle to a supporting player.

A game situation

The session can be developed further by playing a game called "variety box". In a 5 metre square box, put a defender in the middle and two attackers just inside the corners at one end. You stand at the other end with a ball. You throw the ball to one of the attackers. They can only run forward, but can pass if they want. The defender must tackle the first player who receives the ball, no matter whether they have the ball or not. Score points as follows: 1 for a good tackle technique, 1 for a successful tackle (+1 if it is the ball carrier), 1 for a try scored.

The side on tackle

The session

What you tell your players the session is about:

1 Using the side on tackle as an effective defensive tool.
2 Completing the tackle to maximum effect.

What you tell your players to do:

1 Aim to get your head behind the ball carrier's shorts and then drive in with your shoulder.
2 Drive with your legs on contact and wrap your arms around the ball carrier.
3 Land on top of the ball carrier.

What you get your players to do:

Set out a 7 metre square. A ball carrier and a tackler each stand 3 metres behind opposite corners. When you shout "GO", the players run over their corners – the ball carrier to score a try in the middle, the tackler to stop him. Once the tackle is complete, the tackler picks up the ball. Swap the roles and ensure tacklers practise with each shoulder.

The side on tackle in focus

Coach's notes

 ### What to call out

"Keep your eyes on the target – the ball carrier's thigh"

"Wide arms before contact"

"Think – shorts, shoulders, wrap"

"Get your head behind the shorts of the ball carrier"

"Track the attacker – deny him time and space"

 ### What to look for

Tacklers not contacting with their shoulder first and using their arms, so swinging around or even falling off the tackle.

Tacklers not driving with their legs at the tackle and so losing the advantage of the tackle. They must keep their feet on the ground throughout the tackle.

 ### What to think about

What you want your tacklers to do after making the tackle? Get up and challenge for the ball? Do you know the laws? A tackler, once on their feet, can compete for the ball from any angle, unlike any other player. When are your players more likely to make side on tackles? Do you always want your side on tacklers to go for the legs?

Tackling

The side on tackle

direction of run ▪▪➡ ground covered ➡

Developing the session

The training session can be developed as follows.

1 Change the aggressiveness of the runners depending on the players' technical levels.

2 Widen the channel to make the tackler move further to make tackles. This is more tiring, so remind them to concentrate on technique all the time.

A game situation

The session can be developed further by playing a 3 v 1 game. A defender stands on the side of a 10 metre square box, about halfway along. Three attackers line up at one end and attack down the box, with the ball starting with the attacker nearest the defender. The defender has to tackle at least one of the players, scoring more points if they successfully tackle the ball carrier and even more points if they prevent a try being scored. Initially, only allow the attackers to run forward and pass.

The front on tackle

The session

What you tell your players the session is about:

1 Making tackles against opponents running straight at you.
2 Preventing the opposition breaking through the defensive line.

What you tell your players to do:

1 Get your head to one side of the ball carrier and make contact with your shoulders on the bottom of the shorts.
2 Let the ball carrier's momentum take you to the ground and hold on with a tight grip.

What you get your players to do:

Warm-up: With each player on their haunches, with their arms out. Have them fall backwards and to one side. They must turn, land on their front and jump up. Make sure they fall both ways. This will simulate the "falling" when making a front on tackle.

The front on tackle

ground covered ➡

Main practice: In a 2 metre channel, set a tackler on their haunches. A ball carrier jogs forward and falls over a designated shoulder of the tackler. Develop this by increasing the speed of the runner and making sure they attack both shoulders. Eventually have the tackler standing up to tackle proactively.

Coach's notes

 ### What to call out

"Head up, chin off your chest"
"Keep your eyes open throughout the tackle"
"Twist the ball carrier as you fall"
"Hold on tight throughout the tackle"

 ### What to look for

Poor head positions. A key factor not only for safety but also for an effective tackle. The head should be flush against the pocket of the shorts.
Bouncing off the tackle. Tacklers need to bend at the knees and open the arms wide, and then lock onto the target.

 ### What to think about

Can the front on tackle be used more aggressively with the ball carrier driven back? It is recommended that at junior levels, tackles are kept at thigh height. At more experienced levels, the tackler can target the ball. Some players can be taught to step into the tackle, with the front foot and impact shoulder on the same side of the body.

Developing the session

The training session can be developed as follows.

1   Change the aggressiveness of the runner depending on the levels of your players.
2   Have two tacklers in a line, with one tackler going lower than the other.

A game situation

The session can be developed further by playing the "break the line" game. Mark out a 10 metre square box. Three defenders have to defend a line against two attackers with a ball. Keys are communication and good use of the front on tackle. Make sure the tackling team complete the tackle by getting to their feet to contest for the ball. Only once the ball is retrieved by the defenders, or the attackers have scored, is the game over.

The rear tackle

The session

What you tell your players the session is about:

1 Bringing down a player from behind.
2 Covering back to make a tackle.

The rear tackle in focus

What you tell your players to do:

1 Aim to tackle the ball carrier by putting your shoulder into the back of their shorts.
2 Then slide and wrap your arms around their legs and pull tight.

What you get your players to do:

Warm-up: Play a game called "truck and trailer". Split your players into pairs, each pair with a ball. One player without a ball runs away from the other, who has to try to touch them on the shorts with the ball.

Main practice: In a 3 metre channel, 10 metres long, stand a pair of players back to back in the middle. You stand outside the channel. You pass a ball to one player and shout "GO". The ball carrier jogs towards the line, the other chases and tackles.

Coach's notes

 ### What to call out

"Arms wide before the tackle"
"Let your momentum and weight take the ball carrier down"
"Hold on tight"
"Press your head into their body"

 ### What to look for

Tacklers coming off their feet in the tackle. Feet on the ground act as a drag on the ball carrier adding to the effectiveness of the tackle.
Tacklers tackling too high. This often indicates a poor head position and will mean it will take longer to bring the ball carrier down.

 ### What to think about

When are your players most likely to use this type of tackle? Can you get your tacklers to use their momentum to get into a stronger position to compete for the ball once the ball carrier is brought to the ground?

The rear tackle

C = coach

direction of run ■ ■ ■▶   direction of pass ━━▶

Developing the session

The training session can be developed as follows.

1 Allow the ball carrier to run faster.
2 Change the starting distances between the players.

A game situation

The session can be developed further by playing the "balloon burst" game. In 20 metre square box, two defenders stand on an edge facing into the box. Two attackers jog around five metres away from the edge that the defenders are standing on. You stand behind the two defenders. You throw a ball into the box towards an attacker. Once it passes over the defenders, their balloon is burst and they chase the attackers, who have to score over the line at the far end. Adjust the height of the throw and then length of the box according your players' ability.

Handling

Passing and catching

The session

What you tell your players the session is about:

1 Improving passing and catching skills.
2 Passing a rugby ball accurately – and to a player in a better position.

Good hand positions for running

What you tell your players to do:

1 Pass to a moving player.
2 The receiver must reach out towards the ball carrier, with fingers up and elbows bent.
3 The receiver must tell the ball carrier where they want the ball to be passed.

What you get your players to do:

Get your players into groups of three: a ball carrier and receiver (A1 and A2) and a chaser (D). You blow the whistle and the ball carrier starts running, you blow the whistle a second time and the chaser runs after the ball carrier. If and when the chaser touches the ball carrier, the ball carrier has to pass to the receiver. After a couple of passes, swap the players around. Restart the game, but now both attacking players must avoid being touched whilst in possession of the ball.

Coach's notes

 ### What to call out

"Head up"
"Don't pass unless you are certain"
"Fingers up to catch"
"Pass the ball FOR the player, not TO the player"
"Signal with the hands and making eye contact with each other"

 ### What to look for

The weight and height of the pass. The ball should be firm enough to catch, and passed between shorts and shoulder height. Emphasize accuracy.
Communication – both verbal and non verbal. "Pass" is not enough – better to use names, directions, distances.

 ### What to think about

What sort of passes do you want to encourage your players to use? Initially two handed lateral passes, but "short" passes (pops), one-handed passes, looped passes (to go over defenders) are all worth exploring. What words do you want your players to use to communicate?

Handling

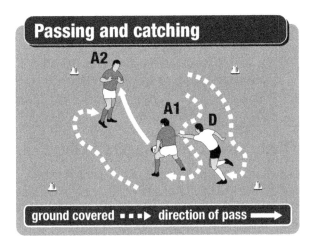

Passing and catching

A2

A1

D

ground covered ■ ■ ■▶ direction of pass ➡

Developing the session

The training session can be developed as follows.

1 Widen the box to encourage longer passes.

2 Allow only a certain type of pass, e.g. spin pass, one-handed or two-handed pass.

A game situation

The session can be developed further by playing the following game. Arrange two teams in a 20 metre square. One team starts with the ball. They must make five passes between them to win a point. Passes can be in any direction and at any height. As soon as they have caught the ball, players must freeze. The defending team must stay 1 metre away from the ball carrier. Possession is turned over if the ball is dropped, intercepted or knocked down.

If the players quickly get the hang of the game, allow the ball carrier to move.

The lateral pass

The session

What you tell your players the session is about:

1 Improving passing speed.
2 Improving catching skills under pressure.

What you tell your players to do:

1 Get your hands up ready for the ball.
2 Use the "hand catch" to keep the ball away from the body.
3 Accelerate onto the ball.
4 Take and give the ball in one smooth action. The sooner you take the ball, the more time you will have.

Good position for hand catch

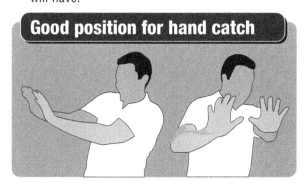

The lateral pass

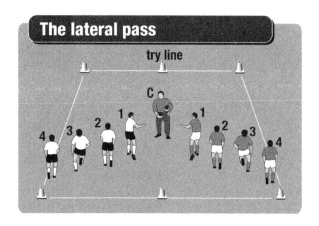

What you get your players to do:

Warm-up: In a static line of four, players pass the ball from one end to the other. The coach times how long it takes to make 12 passes.

Main practice: Two sets of four players line up on either side of the coach. You feed two balls simultaneously to each team's first player. Both teams then run and pass the ball along the line to the outside player (4) who scores a try over the scoring line. The team that scores first wins a point. Teams then swap sides and repeat.

Coach's notes

 What to call out

"Look at the ball"
"Accelerate and keep balanced"
"Reach early for the ball"
"Swing the ball across your body and pass to the receiver's hands"

 What to look for

Players that catch the ball using their hands and body. Encourage players to catch with their fingertips only.

Players who don't reach for the ball early and have to draw the ball back before passing.

 What to think about

Accuracy versus speed, what is the trade off? What should the players do after they have passed the ball? Can spin passes increase or reduce the speed of the line passing for your team?

Developing the session

The training session can be developed as follows.

1 Swap the players around so they appreciate different positions.

2 For older groups, add in miss passes, switches and loops.

3 Add in two defenders to oppose each group.

A game situation

The session can be developed further by playing the following game. Condition a game where the defenders can only defend in a set area of the pitch. Have a 5 metre channel at each side of the pitch which is "out of bounds" for defenders. Load the defence in the middle of the pitch. The ball starts in the centre of the pitch. Encourage the attacking team to move the ball quickly to the outside channels so that scoring is easy.

The spin pass

The session

What you tell your players the session is about:

1 Passing the ball further and quicker using a spin or "torpedo" pass.
2 Knowing when to use the spin pass.

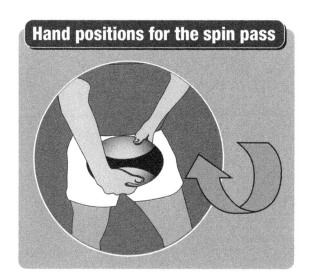

Hand positions for the spin pass

What you tell your players to do:

1 Hold the ball from the underneath and with a "back hand" grip to put the spin on it.
2 Plant the lead foot and lean towards the direction of the pass.
3 Guide the hands to follow through towards the target. Players must understand the importance of the follow through i.e. where the hands follow through to is where the ball will go.

What you get your players to do:

Practice 1: Split the players into pairs with a ball. They stand side by side about 4 metres apart facing forward. The first player holds the ball in his right hand and rests it on the right hip. He turns his body and shoots the ball off the hip towards his partner, the target. He should make sure his hand is towards the target.

Practice 2: Split the players into groups of four or five, standing in a straight line about 5 metres apart. Start the ball at one end. The players must spin pass the ball along the line and back.

Coach's notes

 **What to call out**

"Keep your ball off your body when running"
"Look at the target"
"Pass in front of the target"
"Follow through to the target"

 What to look for

Poor distance with the pass. Get the players to slow down before they pass.

Poor accuracy with the pass. Players should turn their hips towards the intended target to open up the shoulders and better see the receiver.

 What to think about

Why do we need to be able to spin pass? When would you use a spin pass? When would you not use a spin pass? Do your players understand when to use a spin pass?

The spin pass practice 1

Developing the session

The session can be developed as follows.

- Have two lines of players facing each other, start the balls opposite each other – on the whistle it is a race to spin pass the ball along the line and back. This will emphasise the importance of accuracy over speed.

- Have the lines of players jogging and then running in a straight line passing the ball.

- Increase the distance between each player.

A game situation

The session can be developed further by playing the following game. Play 3 v 2 in a 30 metre pitch. This should encourage an accurate pass and the correct pace for the final receiver (who should be running onto the pass, not take it standing still).

The switch pass

The session

What you tell your players the session is about:

1 Using switch passes to beat defenders.
2 Running lines and using dummy passes to create space for the ball carrier.

What you tell your players to do:

1 Ball carrier: change the angle, and attack the defence using a switch or cut pass.
2 Receiver: change the angle once the ball carrier moves into your space.
3 Receiver: run behind the ball carrier, attack the defence, and look to receive a cut pass.

What you get your players to do:

In a 10 metre square box, split one edge into three equal sections. At the other end of the box a ball carrier starts on one corner and a receiver on the

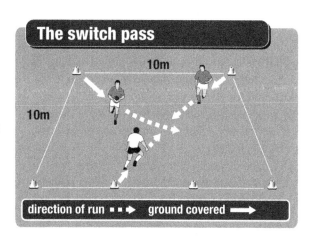

The switch pass

10m

10m

 direction of run ■ ■ ➡  ground covered ➡

other corner. They run forward, with the ball carrier aiming to run into the far section. The receiver runs behind the ball carrier towards the middle section.

Start with no passing to get the timing right. After a couple of goes progress to passing, then onto passing or dummy passing. For the third progression add a defender (as illustrated). Swap starting corners as the drill progresses.

Coach's notes

What to call out

"Draw the opponent by accelerating at their outside shoulder"

"Keep the defender interested by showing and then hiding the ball"

"Receiver: run late and expect the ball"

"Ball carrier: put the ball into the space in front of the receiver"

What to look for

Dropped passes. The receiver must run closer to the passer than usual, give verbal cues and keep their elbows close to their sides (to allow flexibility to receive the pass).

The defender reading the cut. The ball carrier should dummy very early, and attack the defender's far shoulder before the pass. Don't be afraid to allow players to dummy pass.

What to think about

Should a player take contact as they are passing a cut pass? Can your players pass the ball with one hand or do they need to use two? Who calls the switch or cut? Some coaches want both players to call and some just the passer or the receiver. What line do you want your receiver to take after getting the ball?

Developing the session

The training session can be developed as follows.

1 Secretly tell the defender which section to defend.

2 Make the defender more or less "active". In other words, they might rush the ball carrier or just shadow them.

3 Extend the width of the box by 5 metres and add another defender and attacker. The first player with the ball must attack the same section as before.

A game situation

Forcing players to use a switch or cut in a game situation has little merit. Playing a small-sided game where players use switch passes to gain an advantage is preferable. A good game to play is "my rules" touch.

You set the rules, such as the type of touch to make a tackle, and more importantly what is allowed and not allowed in terms of rugby techniques. For instance, turnover the ball if the team in possession performs a bad cut pass. Stop the game to explain the decision (or even better, let the players identify where they went wrong). Give points to sides that "cut" well.

Passing under pressure

The session

What you tell your players the session is about:

1 Passing accurately and at pace when up against a defender.
2 Passing to create overlaps and overloads.

What you tell your players to do:

Attack the defender at pace before giving an accurate pass where the receiver wants it.

What you get your players to do:

In groups of three, one player (P1) controls the exercise, the next (P2) performs a series of skills and a third (P3) acts as receiver. When P1 shouts "GO", he feeds the ball to P2 who attacks a pole or cone. Just before the pole P2 gives a flat pass to P3 who comes onto the ball at pace.

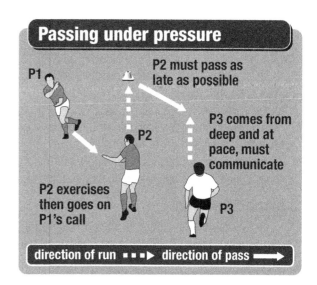

Passing under pressure

P1

P2 must pass as late as possible

P2

P3 comes from deep and at pace, must communicate

P2 exercises then goes on P1's call

P3

direction of run ▪ ▪ ▪▶   direction of pass ━━▶

P2's skills/exercises can include hitting a pad and driving on, press ups and disorientation exercises (spinning round with closed eyes). P1 can also control catching skills, e.g. through random passing.

Coach's notes

💬 What to call out

"Accelerate toward defender"
"Keep the hands high to receive the ball and give the pass"
"Follow your pass, especially when passing further"
"Receiver: communicate and give a target"
"Follow the hands through to the target"
"Receiver: accelerate onto the ball"

🔍 What to look for

Players slowing down to pass too early before defender – the pass must "interest the defender".
Receiver having to adjust to take the pass, e.g. slowing down or reaching behind.

💡 What to think about

Who in the team are these skills most relevant for? How do these skills vary for backs and forwards? How should the passer make allowances for different receivers? Work hard between passes on whatever skills or exercises are being performed.

Developing the session

The training session can be developed as follows.

1 Swap the pole for a defender (possibly with a ruck pad) who varies the pressure put on the passer.

2 The receiver varies the distance of the pass (short or long) and off both sides.

3 Introduce a second receiver (one short and one long) so the passer has to decide who to pass to.

A game situation

The session can be developed further by playing a 3 v 2 game in a wide area. The three players attack the try line and try to score. The two defenders move from side to side along the try line. The attackers attempt to fix the defenders by running straight at them and passing to supporters coming at pace from deep. They should try to give passes as late as possible.

As the players improve allow the defenders to move forward and/or introduce contact. Change the teams around after each score.

Development: Each team stands 5 metres apart. You call for an exercise to be performed and then throw the ball to the attacking side after a short interval.

The clearance pass

The session

What you tell your players the session is about:

1 Passing the ball away from a ruck or maul.
2 Understanding how team mates pass from a ruck and maul, thus aiding players' timing and continuity.

What you tell your players to do:

1 Improve your passing ability and decision making from rucks and mauls and learn your capabilities.
2 Choose options based on the attacking players who are available to pass to.

What you get your players to do:

Set out four cones (lettered A, B, C, D), with the first two cones alongside each other and about

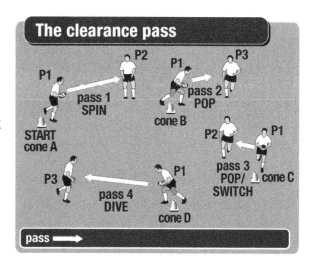

The clearance pass

pass 1 SPIN
pass 2 POP
pass 3 POP/ SWITCH
pass 4 DIVE
START cone A
cone B
cone C
cone D

pass ➡

10 metres apart. Place the next cone forward about 3 metres and the final cone a further 3 metres on.

Starting at cone A with a ball on the floor, one player (P1) makes a long spin pass to another (P2), who puts the ball down at cone B. P1 runs to cone B and

Coach's notes

What to call out

"Sit low in the scrum half position to maintain a stable base"

"Don't step and pass – pass and step"

"Look for the target before you put hands on the ball"

"CHECK your options, DECIDE which is best, EXECUTE a suitable pass"

"Do what your players expect, but not what the opposition expects – in other words, surprise them not us"

What to look for

Poor foot positions. Ideally the ball should be in the middle of the feet for most passes with one foot pointing towards the intended receiver.

Over ambitious passes. The exercise is about learning what is possible. It's better to be safe and get the team going forward than spinning the ball 10 yards.

What to think about

What calls might be used by the passer and receiver to help make the pass more effective – more than just "left/right" or "yes"? In what circumstances will a non-scrum half have to act as a scrum half? Why might your team "pick and go" or "pass and support"? Build a game plan based on your strengths.

pops the ball to another player (P3) who runs to and puts the ball down at cone C.

At cone C, P1 then pops or flicks the ball to P2 who is running from behind P1. He runs to cone D, goes to the ground the wrong way. P1 has to pick out the ball and then dive pass to P3.

Developing the session

The training session can be developed as follows.

1. Have the players pass in both directions (especially the long ones).
2. Make the receivers call for the type of pass they want.
3. Add defenders who might either pressurise the acting scrum half or the receivers.

A game situation

The session can be developed by playing an overload game, with two more players on the attack team. Play the game in a smaller area than normal before expanding the pitch once the players have got the hang of it. Have two non specialists scrum halves in the attack team. Only these players can pick up the ball from a ruck or maul, to "pick and go" or pass. Don't allow scrums or lineouts. Restart the game by throwing the ball to the attack team.

Simple loops

The session

What you tell your players the session is about:

1 Using loops to create an extra man in attack.
2 Passing rapidly and accurately at pace.

What you tell your players to do:

1 Pass the ball and support on the outside of the receiver.
2 Receive the loop pass and exploit the extra man in attack.

What you get your players to do:

Warm-up: Have a group of three players stand in a column, with a ball at the front. When you shout "GO", the column runs forward. The ball carrier steps left, passes right and then runs to join the back of the column. This should continue for 10 metres before the column returns by passing the other way.

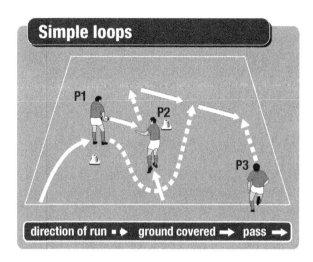

Simple loops

P1 P2 P3

direction of run ▪▶ ground covered ➡ pass ➡

Main practice: In a 10 metre wide box, three players stand in a line at one end. The first player (P1) runs forward, passes to the second player (P2) and then loops. Ideally he should loop without having to run back.

Coach's notes

 What to call out

"Don't loop until you have passed the ball"
"First receiver: move towards pass"
"First receiver: pass the ball into the space for the "looper" to run on to it"
"Third receiver: hold your run longer than normal"

 What to look for

The first receiver slowing down too early. He must attack the inside shoulder of his opposite man to create the real space for the "looper". The quick forward movement will allow the looper to run a better supporting line.
Slow passing. The first pass must be firm. The second pass draws the looper onto the ball, but must be given firmly to avoid interception.

 What to think about

Can the first receiver pass "blind"? How close do you want your looper to get to the first receiver? What angles do you want the third player to run? Can all your players use this move? Can you encourage the first receiver to use the looping player as a decoy and run a dummy move?

Handling

P2 then steps in and passes to P1 as he loops around. The third player (P3) holds his run and then accelerates to meet a pass from the looping player (P1). Use cones to help players understand their running lines.

Developing the session

The training session can be developed as follows.

1   Add defenders to pressure the first two players.
2   Loop to the left, as well as to the right.
3   Add another player who uses a miss pass, before the missed player also loops around.

A game situation

The session can be developed further by playing the following game. Using at least half the width of a normal pitch (the length is not important), set up a game of 4 v 4. Use touch rules, one touch only. This should encourage players to loop to create overlaps. Don't allow switches (cut passes).

Passing to create space

The session

What you tell your players the session is about:

1. Communicating in broken play to find a defensive weaknesses.
2. Moving the ball to the weakness and exploiting it.

What you tell your players to do:

1. All players are responsible for identifying the space to attack.
2. Players need to preserve the space in front of them by using the ball quickly.
3. Don't run toward the space, fix the defenders and move the ball.

What you get your players to do:

Warm-up: Five players in a 30 metre channel have to pass the ball from one side of the channel to the other without moving forward more than 10 metres. Narrow or widen the channel depending on the players' ability.

Main practice: In the same channel, set up two defenders standing 3 metres behind three cones and five attackers, facing away from the cones and 15 metres away from the defenders.

You shout two letters, indicating which two of the three cones spread across the channel the defenders have to run over. At the same time, the attackers turn and receive the ball from you. They then try to beat the defenders.

Coach's notes

 ### What to call out

"Heads up, scan for gaps, look for mismatches, communicate"

"Don't take up the space in front of you if there is space wider"

"Wide men: stay wide – stretch the defence"

"Passers: once you have passed, support on the inside shoulder"

"Support runners: keep your depth and hit the line at pace"

 ### What to look for

Over use of the miss pass. Quick passes are likely to hold defenders. Use a miss pass only to find a runner to break through the defence line.

Players running sideways in the face of tight defence. This is only effective against a spread defence where there are more gaps between the players (assuming the ball carrier is fast enough to exploit the gaps).

If ball carrier is running laterally, make sure support runners hold defenders by running straight.

 ### What to think about

When should players use switch/cut/scissor passes and loops? What calls could you use to quickly get the ball wide or to go for the break through because there is no space wide? Is there a role for a kick behind the defence? How can you effectively use decoy or "option" runners?

Handling

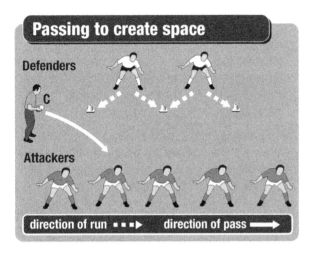

Passing to create space

Defenders

C

Attackers

direction of run ▪▪▪▶   direction of pass ━━▶

Developing the session

The training session can be developed as follows.

1   Set up a wider or narrower channel to attack in.
2   Add more defenders or attackers.
3   More cones or change the starting points for the defenders.

A game situation

The session can be developed by playing the "supersize attack" game. Set up seven attackers and four defenders on nearly the width of a pitch. The teams start about 20 metres apart. You run along the attacking line before releasing the ball to an attacking player to start the game. Depending on the amount of contact required, you can use touch or full tackles. Allow offloads, but not rucks or mauls. The attack has five attempts to score. You could sometimes kick the ball behind the attack to practise counter attacks.

Offloading in contact

The session

What you tell your players the session is about:

1 Creating the opportunity to offload the ball out of a tackle.
2 Penetrating the defence by getting level with the defensive line and beyond before delivering the ball.

What you tell your players to do:

1 Isolate defenders and attack them.
2 Use fast feet to "fix" defender and attack the space either side of them.
3 Get arms free and drive the legs to get beyond the defender.
4 Support needs to arrive at pace on the ball carrier's shoulder.

What you get your players to do:

The ball carrier (A1) attacks the defender (D) and tries to get past. The defender scrags or holds the

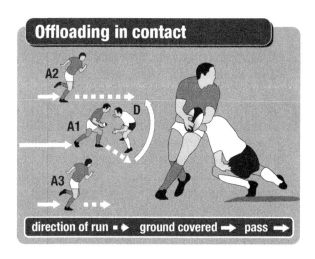

Offloading in contact

direction of run ▪▶   ground covered ➡   pass ➡

ball carrier by the shirt or shorts and gives some resistance. The ball carrier drives through the tackle and then offloads to one of two supporters (A2 and A3) coming from deep and at pace.

The support players must work to get close to the ball carrier and communicate when they want the ball passed. The ball carrier should be able to offload to a player on either side.

Coach's notes

 What to call out

"Attack at pace – step sideways just before contact"
"Attack the sides of the defender not their body"
"Drive the legs through the tackle"
"Hold the ball in two hands. Have hard arms through the tackle, then soft hands for the offload"

 What to look for

Ball carriers not moving defenders – They need to get defenders off balance.
Ball carriers holding the ball under one arm.
Ball carriers not getting beyond the defender.
Offload passes being knocked on due to being forced – if it's not on, hold on!

 What to think about

How far beyond the tackle does the ball carrier need to get? Does the ball carrier always need to hold the ball in two hands? Does the ball carrier need to be able to see the support player he is passing to?
Can we get support players either side of the ball carrier? In what situations would the ball carrier not look to offload?

Developing the session

The training session can be developed as follows.

1 Move on from scrag to full contact and make it competitive between the ball carrier and defender.

2 If the support players are consistently too early have them perform an exercise before they start their runs (for instance three clap press ups then go).

3 Add a second defender 3 metres to the side of the first. The ball carrier has to attack the space between the two defenders and work to get the offload away.

A game situation

"Offload touch" is a good warm-up game to get your players into the mindset of always looking to offload. When the ball carrier is touched he must offload the ball within two seconds to a supporter within 2 metres of them (otherwise it's a turnover). You can build up to scrag rugby. Again the ball carrier must offload within two seconds to a support player close to them.

Finally play full contact games on a narrower pitch where offloads are likely to be an important attacking weapon.

Handling in a narrow space

The session

What you tell your players the session is about:

1 Creating space in a narrow area by changing angles of running.
2 Allowing supporting players to attack space in a narrow area with short passes.

What you tell your players to do:

1 Ball carriers: keep changing your running lines to exploit every bit of space.
2 Receivers: read the ball carrier's movements and be prepared to explode onto the ball.

What you get your players to do:

Set up a long 5 metre channel with four or five players in a line and a ball at the front.

Practice 1: The first player (P1) runs forward then steps outside the channel. He passes the ball back

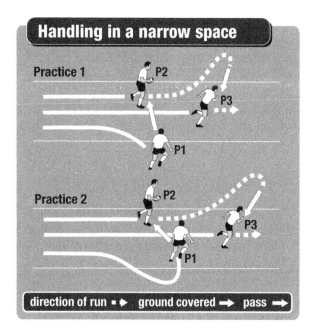

Handling in a narrow space

Practice 1

Practice 2

direction of run ▪▶ ground covered ➡ pass ➡

Coach's notes

 What to call out

"Pass for the supporter, not to them"

"Exaggerate your changes of angle"

"Receivers: hold your run and react to the passers movements"

"Receivers: accelerate onto the ball"

"Passers: give the ball some loop"

 What to look for

Forward passes. The change of angle has meant the passer has turned their shoulders away from the direction of the pass – players should extend their arms in front of their body and flick the wrists to deliver the pass.

Players receiving the ball outside the narrow channel – keep the discipline of the exercise to explore the techniques in more depth.

 What to think about

Should the passer always be using two hands to pass the ball? Is there a need for the receiver to communicate? Who decides whether the pass should be on the left or the right of the passer – can it work differently for different players? What sort of trick passes can be used (for instance, over the shoulder or behind the back)?

Handling

inside and the next player (P2) accelerates onto the ball. This player immediately changes direction to run outside the other edge of the channel and passes the ball back in to the third player (P3). Repeat until every player has passed the ball twice.

Practice 2: Develop by making alternate players go out and back into the channel before passing the ball.

Developing the session

The training session can be developed as follows.

1 Shorten the lengthen of the channel so players have to perform angle changes and passes quicker.

2 Have two channels running side by side, and the players have to run through a different channel after a certain distance.

A game situation

The session can be developed by playing this game. Set up a pitch with four 5 metre channels. Two defenders, one 5 metres behind the other, face four attackers with a ball. Designate an attack channel. The ball must not leave this channel once the attackers have entered. Defenders can move sideways but not backwards or forwards.

Handling and communication

The session

What you tell your players the session is about:

1. Creating spaces between a line of defenders to attack, by revealing "invisible channels".
2. Using good handlers to release good runners.

What you tell your players to do:

1. Ball carriers are going to draw defenders out of position – try to isolate a defender.
2. Release ball level with or behind the defender (if contact is taken).
3. The invisible channel is where the defender was just defending, through and behind them.
4. Supporters are looking to take a pass very close to the defender being attacked.

What you get your players to do:

Mark out three 3 metre channels.

Practice 1: A ball carrier (P1) starts on the far left channel, moves forward then across to the far left channel. The ball carrier then passes the ball back into the middle channel. Another player (P2) starts in the far right channel and then moves into the middle channel to take the ball.

Practice 2: The ball carrier (P1) moves in and out in the far left channel and then passes to the receiver (P2) as he arrives on the shoulder of the ball carrier. The receiver starts in the far right channel.

Coach's notes

 What to call out

"Ball carrier: attack the gaps just beside the defender"

"Attack means going beyond the defender before releasing the ball"

"Drive your legs through the tackle"

"Supporters: put yourselves in the channels by changing angles"

"Supporters: COMMUNICATE"

 What to look for

Attacking players not committing defenders. They need to change direction and accelerate close to contact.

Ball carriers not releasing the ball at the best moment. Passes must be delivered level with or from behind the defender.

Supporters not hitting the gain line at pace.

 What to think about

Two handed or one handed passes which works best? Should the ball carrier always expect the supporter to be in position? What is the best form of calling: "left" or "right" or just the name of the ball carrier?

Handling

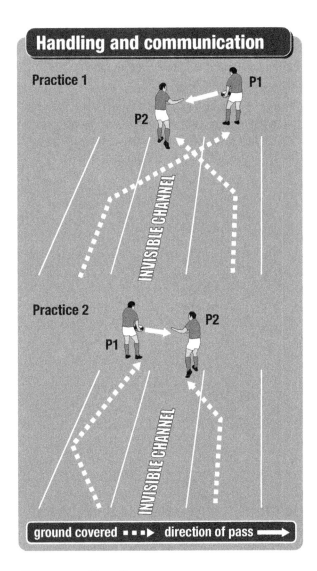

Handling and communication

Practice 1

P2   P1

INVISIBLE CHANNEL

Practice 2

P1   P2

INVISIBLE CHANNEL

ground covered ▪▪▪▶   direction of pass ━━▶

A game situation

"Invisible channels" is an ideal way to create space
where the number of attackers equals the number of
defenders. Use a 3 v 3 or 4 v 4 game. Start the
teams quite a distance apart and see how the play
develops. The ball should start at one edge of the
pitch on a wide pitch.

Picking up the ball

The session

What you tell your players the session is about:

1. Picking up a stationary or moving ball on the ground.
2. Securing the ball either to pass, run or take contact.

What you tell your players to do:

1. Bend at the knees and hips to sweep into the pick up.
2. Place your hands either side of the ball to prevent knock ons.

What you get your players to do:

Warm-up: Pair up your players. Standing side by side, one player rolls out the ball. The second player follows the ball, picks it up and passes it back to their partner.

Picking up the ball

place ball here

direction of run ▪ ▶

Coach's notes

 What to call out

"Get low early, but keep your head up"

"Get into a wide stance over a stationary ball"

"Turn towards the touchline to pick up the ball to present a strong stance"

"Concentrate on securing the ball first, before trying to pass or run"

 What to look for

Players running in too fast to take a clean pick up. Players need to keep the steps short before dipping in. They must aim to remain balanced throughout.

Players knocking on. Ideally, players should have one hand in front and one behind the ball, with the feet either side of the ball.

 What to think about

Can your players pick up the ball with one hand, using a scooping action? Should the players get the ball into the chest straight away, or keep it looser so they can move away quickly? Do you want a stationary ball to be passed straight away, or for the player to start running with the ball? Passing establishes a quicker momentum, but running is less risky.

Handling

Main practice: Arrange a series of columns formed of four players. The first player in each column stands on the touchline with a ball in front. On your signal, this player picks up the ball, runs out 3 or 4 metres, and places the ball on the ground. They turn to become a defender about 2 metres beyond the ball.

The next player in each column picks up the ball and either beats the defender or passes to one of the support players. The defender can try and disrupt the pass to test how strong the player's body position is. The next ball carrier places the ball and becomes the defender and the exercise continues across the width of the pitch.

Developing the session

The training session can be developed as follows.

1   Instead of picking up the ball whilst on the ground, the player has to fall on the ground, gather and stand up.
2   In a separate exercise, roll out a ball which two players chase after. They challenge each other for the ball on the ground.

A game situation

In a 30 metre square, two teams of five play a normal game of touch rugby. Condition it so that if a player is touched, they have to either roll the ball back to a team mate or place it on the ground for a team mate to gather.

If the ball is placed, the team in possession has 3 seconds to pick up the ball and continue to play. If the ball is rolled back, then any player can challenge for it. The first player to get two hands on the ball gains possession and gets to restart with a free pass.

Try scorers

The session

What you tell your players the session is about:

Scoring (and preventing) tries very close to the try line.

What you tell your players to do:

1 Ball carriers must drive forward low and then turn away from contact to get the ball to the ground.

2 Tacklers must work hard to get their bodies and arms between the ball and the ground.

What you get your players to do:

Two players stand facing each other 2 metres apart. There is a line between them. A third player stands at the side with a ball. He throws the ball to one of the players who has 5 seconds to try to put the ball down over the line. The other player tries to save the

try. Adapt the distances between the players according to success. Ensure the three players alternate their roles.

Coach's notes

 What to call out

"Tackler: pull the ball into the ball carrier"

"Tackler: get your hips level and under the ball carrier's hips in the tackle"

"Ball carrier: keep the ball away from your body"

"Ball carrier: twist and roll as you fall"

 What to look for

Too few tries being scored. Ensure that the ball carrier (and supporter if appropriate) gets and maintains forward momentum.

Too many tries being scored. Ensure that the defender drives the ball carrier back and tries to clamp the ball between themselves and the ball carrier.

 What to think about

Do your defenders change the way they tackle depending, on the relative sizes of ball carrier and defender? Can the ball carrier change the height from which they drive for the line and at what stage? Too low and they might lose crucial momentum just before line, too high and they become an easier target to drive back. With two players defending the line, how might they organise to tackle the ball carrier?

Handling

Developing the session

The training session can be developed as follows.

1   Vary the height of the pass – high, low, on the ground.

2   Designate an attacker and let them start with the ball. Stipulate the position they can start in, e.g. with the ball at the feet, or facing away from the defender.

3   Start the defender 1 or 2 metres to the side of the attacker, with the attacker a metre further back from the line, to replicate a saving tackle from a covering player.

4   Allow both players to move along the line, so the defender tracks the attacker until the ball is passed.

5   Set up players in pairs, each with one player standing just behind the partner. Then practice before allowing passes and double tackles.

A game situation

The session can be developed by playing a 3 v 2 game. Form groups of players with three attackers and two defenders. Set up a number of 5 metre square boxes – one for each group – with a try line running through each about 1 metre from one end (put the boxes across a real try line for instance). Place a ball by the side of each box.

The attackers start at the end of the box furthest from the line, faced by the defenders. When you are ready, run to a box and kick or roll the ball in. The attackers must pick up the ball and attempt to score over the line.

After a couple of sets, change the players around, involve previously unused players. Don't use any more than five players at one time.

Footwork

The swerve

The session

What you tell your players the session is about:

1 Improving footwork and balance.
2 Swerving passed defenders to avoid contact.

What you tell your players to do:

1 Read your opponent's movements before acting.
2 Use evasion skills to beat the opponent and get out of the grid.

What you get your players to do:

Introductory practice: Form pairs of players. Players have to get away from their partner. The following partner has to "shadow" the lead player. Work no longer than 10 seconds and swap over roles.

The swerve

1 point

1 point

1 point

1 point

1 point

direction of run ▪▶   ground covered ➡

Coach's notes

 What to call out

"Hold the ball in two hands"
"Accelerate and keep balanced"
"Stay upright"
"Drive off one foot to change direction"
"Quick feet"

 What to look for

Players who have difficulty changing direction. They can use smaller steps or changes of pace.

Players who always move in the same direction. Ask them to beat the defender on both sides.

 What to think about

How the players can keep their balance while changing direction? What impact does the defender have by changing his lines of running (angles)? How does a change of pace by the ball carrier affect the outcome? What parts of the feet make contact with the ground for a sharp and a smooth change of direction? For the swerve move, try getting players to lean over, and so far one way, that they fall over onto the foot they need to drive-off from in the new direction.

Footwork

Main practice: Mark out a 10 metre box with a 4 metre box in the middle. Put a ball carrier (A) in one corner and a defender (D) on the opposite line. When the ball carrier moves, the defender on the opposite side can move. The ball carrier scores a point if they can get out of the 10 metre box having touched the ball down in the 4 metre box the small square in the centre, without being tackled by the defender. Start with a touch or tag tackle, then move onto a contact tackle.

Developing the session

The training session can be developed as follows.
1   Let the defender move before the ball carrier.
2   Pass or roll the ball to the ball carrier as they move into the box.
3   Change the starting position for attackers and defenders.
4   Change the emphasis of the practice onto the defender.

A game situation

The session can be developed further by playing the following game. Mark out three boxes of widths 10 metres, 20 metres and 30 metres. Organise players into teams of four and play. Start in the 30 metre box where there is plenty of space, move to the 20 metre box then the 10 metre box.

By rotating the players into the different sized playing areas, you are testing their evasion ability in different situations. They will more easily transfer these skills into a full-sided game.

The side step

The session

What you tell your players the session is about:

1   Using side steps and swerves to beat defenders.
2   Keeping balanced during a change in direction.

What you tell your players to do:

Attack one side of the cone or player and drive off hard in the other direction.

What you get your players to do:

Four columns of players stand opposite each other about 10 metres apart, with a ball carrier at the front. Place a diamond shape of cones in the middle (about 1 metre apart). The player at the front of the queue runs to the right of the cone in front of them. They then step or swerve left and accelerate through to the other side. After four attempts by each player, change the direction of the step or swerve. Start very slowly and build up the pace.

The side step

direction of run ▪▶   ground covered ➡

Coach's notes

 What to call out

"Hold the ball in two hands"
"Accelerate away"
"Drive-off from one foot to change direction"
"Dip your shoulder one way and move in the opposite direction"

 What to look for

Players who stop or slow down. They can try a smooth change
of direction rather than a sharp change.

 What to think about

How the players can keep their balance while changing direction. Using "chin-knee-toe" for sidesteps – when making the step, the chin, knee and toe of the driving side should all be in line.

Developing the session

The training session can be developed as follows.

1 Swap the cones for static players.
2 Have a feeder at the start so the players receive a pass as in a game.
3 Have two players run out together, one with a ball. After they step and accelerate, the ball carrier pops the ball to the other player.

A game situation

The session can be developed further by playing the following small-sided game, 4 v 4, to develop the players' evasion skills. A wide playing area should be used to help the players to develop these skills. There is then plenty of space between the defenders for the attacking players to use their evasion skills.

Each side should start at least 15 metres apart. You start each game by throwing the ball to one side. As your players improve, reduce the pitch width. This will reduce the space between the defenders. Use tackling when appropriate.

Improving evasion skills

The session

What you tell your players the session is about:

1 Using footwork to avoid contact.
2 Using footwork to find the spaces between defenders.

What you tell your players to do:

1 Use changes in speed, sidesteps or swerves to beat a defender.
2 Avoid contact with defenders, or reduce defenders' effectiveness in making contact with you.

What you get your players to do:

In a 10 metre square box spread out as many cones, pads and rolled up clothes as possible. Put three players on each corner of the box. A player with a ball from each corner has to cross over as fast as possible without bumping into another player or stepping on something on the ground. Once on the other side, they hand over the ball to the next player.

Gauntlet game

Coach's notes

 What to call out

"Aim for spaces not faces"
"Attack the 'branches and twigs', not the 'tree trunk'"
"Keep your head up for balance and to see"
"Two hands on the ball to keep the defence guessing"

 What to look for

Evasion happening too late. Make players aware that defenders move forward as well as sideways, so cutting down the space.
Evasion is too confused. Players should be strong in their convictions. Too many steps can reduce momentum and make it easier to tackle the ball carrier.

 What to think about

All players need to be able to use good footwork. This means changes of angle and speed to put the ball carrier in a better position to beat an opposition player. Footwork is not just about beating one player in the open, it is also about squeezing through gaps in defences.

Developing the session

The training session can be developed as follows.

1   Add more starting points along the sides of the box.
2   Create a small square in the middle through which no player can go.

A game situation

The session can be developed further by playing the following games.

"**1 v 1 v 2**": In a 20 metre long, 10 metre wide box place one defender in the middle of the box and two defenders at the back of the box. You pass the ball to an attacker who has to try to beat the first defender. If successful, the attacker then tries to beat the last two defenders who are only allowed to move forward 2 metres. Allow full tackling.

"**Gauntlet**": In a 6 metre channel, a player carrying a ball has to run from one end to the other getting past defenders, without being pushed out of the channel. The defenders stand every 5 metres in the channel and try to push the runner out using their arms only, not shoulders. Ideally the defenders use rucking pads.

More advanced evasion skills

The session

What you tell your players the session is about:

1 Using a range of evasion skills to beat defenders.
2 Finding space in front and to the side of defenders.

What you tell your players to do:

1 Accelerate into the grid.
2 Use side steps and/or swerves.

What you get your players to do:

Introductory practice: Set players in pairs, facing each other. Using quick feet movements, each player has to get behind and face their partner's back to win.

Main practice: Lay out a 10 metre square box. Line up attackers facing defenders across the box. When the ball carrier (A) moves, the defender (D) on the opposite side can move. The attacker scores 2 points if they can get to the opposite side of the box and 1 point if they manage to get out either side of the box without being tackled by the

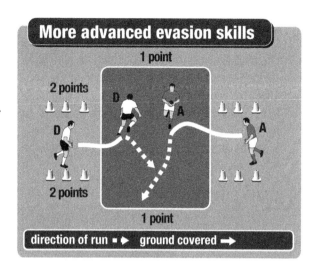

defender. Start with a touch or tag tackle then move onto a contact tackle.

Coach's notes

 What to call out

"Hold the ball in two hands"
"Accelerate and keep balanced"
"Drive off one foot to change direction"
"Dip your shoulder one way and move in the opposite direction"

 What to look for

Players that have difficulty changing direction. Smaller steps before direction change. Players that stop or slow down. Try a smooth change of direction rather than a sharp change.

 What to think about

How the players can keep their balance while changing direction. What impact does the defender make to the attacker by moving forward slowly or quickly? Are the players planning what to do before they start or are they reacting to the defenders'

Footwork

Developing the session

The training session can be developed as follows.

1   Reduce the size of the box to challenge the attackers even more.
2   Pass or roll the ball to the attackers as they move into the box.
3   Start the attackers in a corner and only have the other side line as one point.

A game situation

The session can be developed further by playing a small sided, 4 v 4 game. To assist the players develop these skills, a wide playing area should be used so that there is plenty of space between the defenders for the attacking players to use their evasive skills. As they improve, reduce the pitch width and therefore the space between defenders. Use tackling when appropriate.

Kicking

The punt

The session

What you tell your players the session is about:

1. Kicking in open play under pressure.
2. Pressurising the kicker and charging down poor kicks.

What you tell your players to do:

1. Keep the ball in the middle of your body.
2. Strike through the ball so your leg does not go across the ball.

What you get your players to do:

Warm-up: Two players stand 5 metres apart and kick to each other alternating between feet. Increase the distance once the players are kicking accurately.

Main practice: Three players stand in a line at the corner flag. You roll the ball out into the playing

The body position to kick the ball

area. One player chases after the ball, retrieves it and passes it to another player who has to punt the ball through the posts. The third player runs along the line for 15 metres and then turns infield to put pressure on the kicker only.

Coach's notes

 What to call out

"The direction of your shoulders is the direction of the kick"

"Drop the ball and watch it onto your foot"

"Strike the ball on your laces and point your toes"

"Defender: get your hands up early with your arms in front of your head"

 What to look for

The ball coming off the side of the foot. Is the ball being dropped outside the middle of the body or is the kick across the ball? Either can give inconsistent results. They may be okay for some kicks, but not every time.

The kicker being charged down too often. How many steps is the player taking before they make the kick? Three should be the maximum.

 What to think about

The height of the kick depends on the position of the ball in relation to the player's body when it is kicked. Do your defenders know which of the kicker's feet is the strongest? Can your kickers change kicking foot to avoid being charged down? Do you want to try the "drop punt", where the kicker strikes the ball on its point? It is a variation of the Aussie Rules method of kicking and works better for some players.

Kicking

The punt

15m

direction of kick ▪► ground covered ➡ pass ➡

A game situation

The session can be developed by playing "penalty touch", a game to improve the length and accuracy of punts. Pair up your players. One player stands 15 metres from the halfway line. He kicks for touch as if from a penalty. If the kick makes touch, the second player takes the ball from the point it went into touch, walks in 15 metres and returns the kick. If the ball does not make touch, then the original kicker has to retire 20 metres to kick again. The winner is the player who forces the ball to go out on their kick on their opponent's 5 metre line. Repeat the game with the second player starting. Then change ends and start again.

The grubber kick

The session

What you tell your players the session is about:

1 Increasing attacking options through grubber kicks (kicks along the ground).
2 Turning and getting behind a flat defence which is closing you down quickly.

What you tell your players to do:

1 Only kick through a gap or through an angle.
2 Attack the defence and kick as late as possible.
3 Use the outside foot and drop the ball onto the foot.
4 Point the toe down on contact and strike the upper half of the ball.
5 Chaser: stay low, kick ahead if you need to, drop on the ball to score or sweep it up to run on.

What you get your players to do:

Set out a 5 metre wide by 10 metre long box.

Practice 1: The ball carrier stands at one corner and grubber kicks the ball for another player, standing at the adjacent corner, to chase. The chaser picks up the ball and both players run through the box. Repeat with the players swapping places.

Practice 2: The ball carrier (A1) runs at an angle from the corner of the box, and then kicks for the other player (A2) to chase. Repeat the practice as before.

Practice 3: Starting at the side of the box, the ball carrier (A1) runs forward and kicks for two players (A2, A3) to chase. A defender (D) must try to block the kick, first with just their legs only, and then by any means.

Coach's notes

 What to call out

"Keep your head and knee over the ball, lean forward so there is less loss of momentum"

"Strike through the upper section of the ball – unless you can see the centre of the ball, you are not doing it right"

"Chasers: keep onside and follow the line of the ball"

"Kick on your laces"

 What to look for

Not kicking the ball below the knee height of the opposition, where there is less to get in the way of the ball.

Kickers slowing down too much before kicking and so giving away their intentions to the defenders.

 What to think about

Should the ball be picked end-on-end so it pops up, or kicked so it rolls along the floor? What are the advantages of using the side or the top of the foot? Who calls for the grubber or do players just react to it? Can you use a grubber in defence as well as attack? What sort of defence would be best to use a grubber against?

Kicking

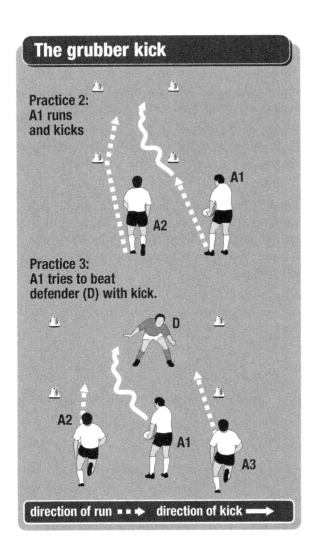

The grubber kick

Practice 2:
A1 runs
and kicks

A1

A2

Practice 3:
A1 tries to beat
defender (D) with kick.

D

A2

A1

A3

direction of run ▪ ▪ ➤   direction of kick ➜

Developing the session

The training session can be developed as follows.

1   Add another defender. The attackers can only
    score by kicking through and recovering the ball.

2   Start the defenders and attackers at each side of
    the box. They have to run around the corners
    before playing as the previous development.

The chip and chase

The session

What you tell your players the session is about:

1 Increasing attacking options against a flat defence.
2 Communication between players, the chipper and chaser.

What you tell your players to do:

1 Fix the defender by feinting and start to draw the tackle.
2 Drop the ball onto the foot so your stride is not broken.
3 Kick the ball on its point to get height quickly.
4 Keep your head down over the ball.
5 Chaser: try to gather the ball on the full. Run where you think the ball will land, not behind it.

What you get your players to do:

The following three practices can be used to build the techniques and skills required.

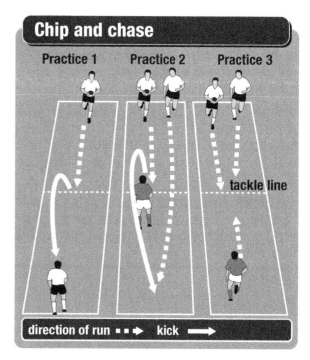

Chip and chase

Practice 1   Practice 2   Practice 3

tackle line

direction of run ▪ ▪ ➔   kick ➡

Coach's notes

 What to call out

"Keep the ball in the middle of the body"

"Slow down to kick. The chaser will add the acceleration"

"Chaser: stay deep. The kicker will slow down"

"Chaser: don't expect the kick to happen or work. Be prepared to support in other ways"

 What to look for

The kicker chipping too early, enabling the defender to turn and chase. The kicker needs to interest the defender with feints and dummies.

The chaser overrunning the kicker. The chaser should accelerate as the kick happens, not before.

 What to think about

Where on the field this type of kick should be used? Is it going to be a pre-planned move? Can the kicker angle the kick to use chasers coming from different directions? Does the chip always have to be gathered on the full or can it be allowed to bounce?

Kicking

Practice 1: The simple chip. The player moves forward to the tackle line and aims a chip kick (no higher than just over the cross bar of the rugby posts) to a receiver waiting 10 metres away. The receiver gathers and they swap places.

Practice 2: The chip over a static defender. A chaser runs alongside the kicker and tries to gather the chip before the ball reaches a line 10 metres away. The defender can jump to block as the players develop.

Practice 3: The chip and chaser "live". A defender and two attackers start 20 metres apart in a channel no wider than 3 metres. The two attackers have to beat the defender. If the ball is chipped, it is allowed to go outside the channel.

Developing the session

The training session can be developed by making the channel wider and having two defenders and three attackers.

A game situation

The session can be developed further by playing the following game. Set up two teams in a box with the ball in a ruck, maul or scrum. The ball is passed out. The attack has one chance to break down the opposition line. They can use any normal form of attack, though if this results in a ruck or maul deem the attack to have ended. Mark out three "chip" zones. Defenders are not allowed into these zones. If an attacker can chip the ball into a zone and a chaser gathers it, then the team automatically scores a point. If a try is then scored, another point is scored. The "chip" zones can be designated by the attacking side.

The place kick

The session

What you tell your players the session is about:

1 Improving conversion and penalty kicking accuracy and distance.

What you tell your players to do:

1 Concentrate on striking the ball on the "sweet spot".
2 Follow through with the kick to the target.

The "sweet spot"

The best place to strike the ball with the foot is about a third of the way up the ball on a seam. The shape of the ball fits the foot.

Your players need to experiment to find out what point feels most comfortable. They must keep their eyes focused on this point in their run up.

The place kick

Ball angled, kicking on the point

Ball upright, kicking just below the middle

Coach's notes

 What to call out

"Plant the foot in line with the ball"
"Kick on the laces of the boot"
"Have a "hard" front toe"
"Keep the non-kicking side arm out"

 What to look for

A lack of distance. The player may not be driving the foot through the ball, probably because the kicker is leaning back or their hips are not in line with the posts

A lack of accuracy. The kicker may not be balanced at the point of impact. Check the arms and head position. Are these correct? Is the kicker going through the same routine before every kick?

 What to think about

The angle and height of the ball on the kicking tee. What is most comfortable for your kicker?

Kicking

What you get your players to do:

Put a ball on tee or cone. Aim a seam towards the target. Place the non kicking foot next to the ball and step a couple of paces backwards and to the side. Look at the sweet spot, then the target. Breathe in and then out. Jog towards the ball, keeping your eyes on it. Plant the non kicking foot in line with the ball. Keep the arm on the side of the non-kicking foot horizontal for balance. Kick through the ball towards the target.

Practice 1: Put a rucking bag or tackle pad 1 metre in front of the kicking tee. The kicker practises hitting kicks into the pad to improve rhythm.

Practice 2: The kicker stands on the try line, facing one post. They aim to hit it from various distances.

Developing the session

A game situation

The session can be developed by playing the "goal kick competition". The first player puts the ball next to the kicking tee. He then runs around the posts and has 45 seconds to tee up, step back and kick the goal. Repeat for each player, recording the times and scores.

Development: For conversion type kicks, have a defending player try to charge down the kick. Have another player 10 metres away shouting at the kicker to put extra pressure on the kicker.

The drop kick

The session

What you tell your players the session is about:

1 Taking a drop kick restart.
2 Drop kicking for points.

What you tell your players to do:

1 For the restart, aim to hang the ball in the air by leaning back a little and striking through the ball.
2 For the drop goal, offset the shoulders just outside target, lean forward and drive the leg through the ball.

What you get your players to do:

Warm-up – dropping the ball: The player stands in the kicking position and drops the ball so it bounces up and he can scoop it up with his hands.

Practice 1 – kick off: Two players stand 20 metres apart. They drop kick the ball to each other. They concentrate on accuracy rather than distance.

The drop kick

Coach's notes

 What to call out

"Drop the ball from below hip height"

"Keep your eyes focused on the ball at all times"

"Make your toes "hard" (point them, for example) and strike the ball on the laces of the boot"

"Follow through with the leg"

 What to look for

The leg action. The kick should always be through the ball. For the drop goal, the leg should travel forward with the whole body. For the restart, it should go through and up.

The drop. The ball needs to be upright and dropped so it bounces back slightly.

 What to think about

Restart long or short? What's the team's strategy? What's your drop goal strategy? Who should be practising drop goals – the number eight, scrum half, full back, centres and wings? When might they use the skill? The ground conditions. The rebound of the ball off the ground prior to the kick needs to give the kicker some lift.

Kicking

Remember that the foot needs to be hard on contact and the toe pointed up slightly. Reduce and increase the distances, but ensure the kicker lands the ball very close to the receiver to replicate a game situation.

Practice 2 – drop goal: Set up three players, the kicker, a passer and a defender behind the goal posts. The kicker receives a pass and kicks for goal. The players then rotate. The pass should be challenging so the kicker has to correct themselves to find a rhythm to go for goal. The defender can charge down the kick if appropriate.

Developing the session

A game situation

The session can be developed further by playing the "pressure kick" game. You stand on the 22 metre line in front of the goal posts with three players. You roll the ball out. One player chases after the ball and then passes it back towards another player who gets into position to kick a drop goal. The third player runs around the ball as it is rolled out, without interfering with the pass, and then tries to charge down or prevent the kicker making a successful drop goal attempt.

Catching a high ball

The session

What you tell your players the session is about:

1 Catching high balls under pressure.
2 Supporting and moving the ball away from danger.

What you tell your players to do:

1 Call clearly and move into position early.
2 Reach up for the ball. Turn towards the nearest touchline.
3 Support players must work hard to get behind the catcher to provide options.
4 If there's pressure, move the ball away from the catching zone. Otherwise, pop the ball to a supporter or prepare to maul.

What you get your players to do:

Practice 1: In a small grid, a player throws a high ball. A receiver calls for the ball, catches it and pops

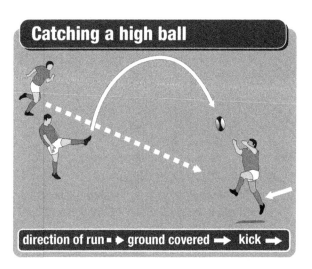

Catching a high ball

direction of run ▪ ▶ ground covered ➡ kick ➡

it to another player. This continues, with each player having a number of throws, catches and pop passes. Develop by making the thrower put pressure on the catcher. The supporter now has to make a decision on whether to take a pop pass or drive in on the catcher.

Coach's notes

 What to call out

"Call early and make it your ball" – confidence is vital under pressure

"Jump to take the catch – you can't be "tackled" in the air"

"Keep the legs a shoulder width apart" – this allows players to move off quickly or take contact

"Supporters: keep deep and behind the catcher so they can see you. Look forward and tell them where you are going"

 What to look for

Players losing focus on the ball. They should keep their eyes on manufacturer's name.

Players not turning their body sideways.

Players not bringing the ball into their body after they catch it.

 What to think about

When might you catch the ball on the run? What are the catcher's options: kick, pass, run? Should the catcher have two feet on the ground or jump for the ball? Calling the mark – is it always worth it? A counter attack strategy: kick, run back, pass and kick? Catching like an Aussie Rules player (reverse hands) or cradling (like a baby)? How should players use the elbows and fingers?

Kicking

Practice 2: In a larger grid, one player kicks to a catcher with a support player. Another chases the kick. The catching team tries to beat the chaser and then the kicker.

Developing the session

The training session can be developed as follows.
1   Add more chasers and supporters.
2   Change the size of the grid, making the chasers either further away or closer to the kicker and/or the catcher.
3   Change the type of kick, e.g. box kick, bomb, drop kick.
4   Make the supporters start in front of the catcher.

A game situation

Develop the session with these game situations and their typical catchers: a drop out (any forward); a box kick (the no. 8 or a winger); a high ball (the full back or a winger). The scrum half or fly half kicks into a designated area on the pitch where these situations might occur (the kick does not have to be perfect). The players start from set positions (e.g. lineout, second phase breakdown). Play through the situation and get quick feedback. Play again and then swap attackers and defenders. Focus on the session objectives, but allow players to make their own decisions. Develop the practice by halving the pitch size and the number of players.

The ruck

What is a ruck?

The session

What you tell your players the session is about:

1 Understanding the laws of the ruck.
2 Setting up a ruck correctly.

What is a ruck?

A ruck is a phase of play where one or more players from each team, who are on their feet, and in physical contact, close around the ball on the ground. Open play has ended.

Players in a ruck may use their feet only to try to win or keep possession of the ball, without being guilty of foul play.

What you tell your players to do:

Practise forming rucks and rucking.

1 Use pictures to show what a ruck should look like. Indicate where the offside line is.
2 Use a question and answer session to develop an understanding of the laws.

A player:

- Must join a ruck from the hindmost feet of their hindmost team mate.
- Must bind with a full arm.
- Cannot use their hands in the ruck.
- Cannot put their feet on another player in the ruck.
- If on the ground, must make every effort to move away from the ball.

Coach's notes

 What to call out

"Stay on your feet in the ruck"
"Join from behind the back feet"
"Remember to keep your shoulders above your hips"
"No hands on the ball"

 What to look for

Players not balanced when entering the ruck. They must stay on their feet, and not fall on the ground.
Players not entering from the hindmost feet.

 What to think about

How many players do you want to enter a ruck? Which players in your team should practise rucking the most – forwards and inside backs?

The ruck

Offside at the ruck

A successful end of a ruck is when:

- The ball leaves the back of the ruck.

An unsuccessful end of a ruck is when:

- The ball becomes unplayable. A scrum is awarded to the team moving forward before the end of the ruck.

Offside at the ruck

A player has to join a ruck from behind the hindmost foot of his own side. Players cannot loiter in front of the hindmost foot.

Core ruck skills

The session

What you tell your players the session is about:

1 Driving out opposition players from the ruck quicker.
2 Securing good, quick ball for the scrum half.

What you tell your players to do:

1 Arrive at a ruck in a position to drive an opposition player backwards.
2 Have a body angle on arrival to keep you on your feet.
3 Aim to drive on and grab an opposition player's "hook" (an arm or leg) or "handle" (shorts, pockets or shirt).

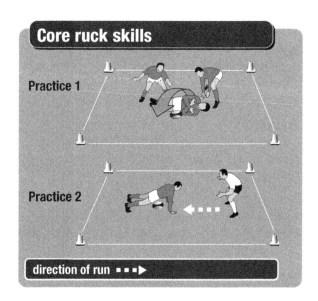

Core ruck skills

Practice 1

Practice 2

direction of run ▪ ▪ ▪▶

Coach's notes

 ### What to call out

"Chin off your chest, helps keep your head up"

"Look over your eyebrows to keep your back horizontal to the ground"

"Take short steps before contact to keep balanced"

"Target one opponent"

"Drive through and out to clear the ruck"

 ### What to look for

Players not focusing on the ball. Driving out opponents should be to free up the ball, not clear out players for the sake of it.

Miss hits at the contact area. Players should keep their eyes open and put the same foot forward as the shoulder with which they make contact.

Players falling over at the ruck. Are they approaching too fast and off balance? Emphasise "low to high" body positions at the point of contact.

 ### What to think about

Should ruckers bind with each other before contact? Does this work for your players? Do you want your players to drive beyond the ball or simply stand over and protect it? How do players know if they should go into a ruck or not? If a player arrives at a ruck and the ball has already been won, what are the options?

The ruck

What you get your players to do:

Practice 1: One player lies on his side on the ground and puts a ball in front of him no more than 1 metre from his hips. Two players, starting 3 metres away, have to lift and roll him over the ball.

Practice 2: One player makes a bridge shape with the ball under their hips. Another player, starting 2 metres away, has to drive the player backwards, by focusing on a hook or handle.

Practice 3: Set up four situations across the pitch where a team of four players has to perform a combination of practices 1 and 2 in the fastest time.

Developing the session

The training session can be developed as follows.

1 Add more defenders into each situation.
2 Use ruck shields, held so they are touching the ground, to get players lower in the contact area.
3 In practice 2, place a "tackled" player next to the ball.

A game situation

The session can be developed by playing the following game. In a narrow playing area, say 20 metres wide, divide your players into two teams with two extra players on the attacking side. Give the attacking side the ball. They have to score at one end of the pitch. They are allowed three "rucks", which can only last three seconds on your count, otherwise the attacks fail. Allow plenty of time for rest between attacks and change the players around regularly. Develop the game by widening the pitch significantly.

Ruck attack

The session

What you tell your players the session is about:

1 Producing good ball to attack the fringes of a ruck.
2 Having an option to restart the forward momentum of a slow attack.

What you tell your players to do:

1 Communicate your intention to support players.
2 Have a low to high body position from the pick up.
3 Keep the ball secure from the opposition.
4 The second player into the ruck needs to be in a driving position, but focused on the ball at all times.

What you get your players to do:

Start this practice in slow motion. Put a player in a press up position over the ball to indicate the back feet of a ruck. Another player picks up the ball and goes around the side of the ruck, with two players in support. Two other players defend passively.

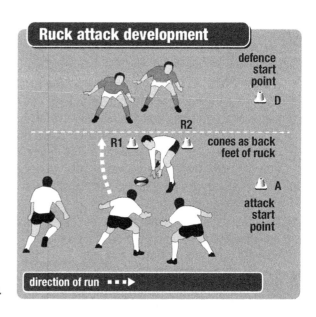

Ruck attack development

defence start point
D
R2
R1 — cones as back feet of ruck
A
attack start point

direction of run ■ ■ ■▶

Develop the session by encouraging the attackers to "pick and go" using the low body position technique, before getting the players to develop a mini-maul.

Coach's notes

What to call out

"Don't get isolated: only carry the ball if sure of support"

"Turn early in tight situations, but always look to go forward"

"Supporters: keep lower than the ball carrier"

"Avoid heavy contact: aim at the arms not the bodies of defenders"

"First supporter: secure the ball"

What to look for

Players standing up immediately with the ball rather than moving from a low position.

Players looking to make choices based on what is in front of them.

Players looking at (scanning) the defence as they approach the ruck.

What to think about

Do you have specific calls when you perform a ruck? When is the best time to pick and go, when to maul? What are the roles of your scrum half and backs? How close to the ruck should the attack be? Where on the field is it best to use this strategy?

Developing the session

The training session can be developed as follows.

1 Allow defenders to tackle and compete for the ball.

2 As the illustration, attackers and defenders approach from cones A and D respectively to vary the angles. Have a player stand by cones R1 and R2 (the "ruck") to release the ball at different times to replicate quicker or slower ball.

3 Add a second ruck position, so the players need to ruck more than once.

4 Make the defenders arrive at different times, so the attackers need to make more decisions on when to ruck and what tactics to use.

A game situation

The session can be developed further by playing the following game. Set up three channels, each less than 10 metres wide, and two teams, each with few players. Starting in the middle channel, the attacking side, who always keep the ball, move forward. When tackled, they need to form a ruck and attack once more in the same channel. They then need to attack into one of the other channels. They recycle and attack again in this channel. Finally they need to attack the channel they have not entered, attacking much wider out. Increase the intensity of the game by allowing the defenders to compete for the ball. Develop the game further by allowing attackers and defenders to move across channels.

Ruck defence

The session

What you tell your players the session is about:

1 Guarding the fringes of the ruck from close attacks, such as "pick and go", or pop passes.
2 Taking the defence to the attack.

What you tell your players to do:

1 Take responsibility for guarding the fringes.
2 The first two players take up position low and very tight to either side of the ruck.
3 The third player covers the side the attack is most likely to happen.
4 The defence moves forward low and aggressively.
5 With more than four players, one player must defend the middle of the ruck.

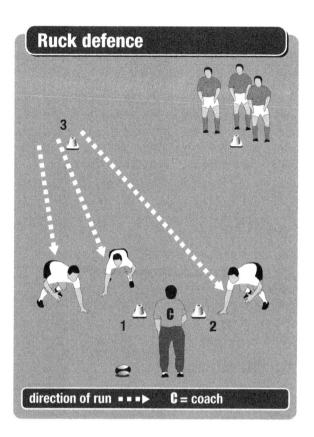

Ruck defence

direction of run ■ ■ ■▶   C = coach

Coach's notes

 What to call out

"Keep balanced, look ahead and stay onside: no penalties."
"Pressurise by shouting" (e.g. blindside covered)
"React to the danger: where are the gaps beside the ruck?"
"Communicate with the player beside you"
"Make tackles back into the ruck"

 What to look for

Players ball-watching rather than reacting to the attackers. Lazy players just filling up the defence where it is easiest. The defenders must communicate, spead out to defend the next phase and take individual responsibility.

 What to think about

Should the defence "go up and out", i.e. move forward and then drift with the pass? What role does the defending scrum half have to play and where should he stand? What type of tackle should the close defence use? Should there be sanctions in the practice for offside? Calls – what do the players shout when the ball comes out of the ruck?

The ruck

What you get your players to do:

You stand behind cones 1 and 2, representing the back feet of a ruck. Place a ball behind one of the cones.

A group of three players at cone 3 run towards you. Two head to the danger area in front of the ball and, one to the other side. All take up a defensive stance. When you touch the ball again, all three players call "HIT" and run forward. Repeat for other groups.

Developing the session

The training session can be developed as follows. Use more than one set of cones to represent the different rucks, so the players have to react to difficult angles, even running backwards or sideways to a set of cones. Then add players to attack the ball-side, and after that more defenders.

A game situation

The session can be developed further by playing the following game. Divide your players into two teams. Set up a 10 metre wide pitch of any length. One team attacks and always wins the ball back. The other team defends. They cannot give away any penalties or compete for the ball on the floor.

Spread the attackers and defenders up and down the pitch. You throw the ball to an attacker who walks forward and is tackled. One player from each side forms a ruck over the ball. The attackers start the attack on your call. In the meantime the defence needs to organise itself. When the game breaks down, restart the same way.

Ruck scan

The session

What you tell your players the session is about:

1 Learning to make quick decisions at the ruck.
2 Improving body positions and angles when arriving at the ruck.

What you tell your players to do:

1 Look at the ruck situation and decide whether you are going to drive through, protect or stay out.
2 If you are going to enter the ruck, go through the "gate", not in at the side.

What you get your players to do:

In the middle of a 7 metre square set out four cones in a rectangle, three strides wide, by two deep. This represents the tackle "gate". Players cannot enter from the sides of this box. Place a ball in the middle of the cone box.

Split the players into teams of four and two and put

Ruck scan

direction of run ■ ■ ▶

them outside the square. When you shout "GO", both teams enter the square and try to win the ball. The team with four players has to work out how many players they want to commit to the ruck.

Coach's notes

 ### What to call out

"Hips below shoulders"
"Eyes open in contact"
"Drive over the ball"
"Take out a defined target"

 ### What to look for

Too many or too few players going into the ruck. Allow players to learn through trial and error with regular breaks for feedback and Q&A to enhance their understanding. Ineffective players at the ruck. Are their techniques right? Low body positions before impact, heads up to focus on the target, and a shoulder into the chest of their opponent?

 ### What to think about

How many players do you want to compete for the ruck ball (think defence and attack)? Do you want players to "ruck over and stay" or "ruck over and through the ball?" Ruck decisions are a balance of careful judgement and then making the maximum impact over the ball. Can your players distinguish between the two? Can your defenders slow the ball legally by their decisions at the ruck?

Developing the session

The training session can be developed as follows.

1   Add players to both teams.
2   Put two players from each team in the square and an equal numbers of attackers and defenders outside (and perhaps make the square bigger).
3   Develop second phase attacks.

A game situation

The session can be developed further by playing a 10 v 10 game (depending on how many players you have) on half a pitch. Use passive five man scrums, allow kicking, and if the ball goes into touch have a contested two man lineout. For penalty offences, have a free kick with the opposition standing 5 metres back. Otherwise normal rugby laws apply except you judge whether players are making a difference at the ruck.

Blow the whistle and question players if necessary. Have any spare players shout judgements from the sidelines. Change the teams to involve all players.

The maul

What is a maul?

The session

What you tell your players the session is about:
1 Understanding the laws of the maul.
2 Building a legally correct maul.

What you tell your players to do:
Practise forming mauls and mauling.
1 Use pictures to show what a maul should look like. Indicate where the offside line is.
2 Use a question and answer session to develop an understanding of the laws.

A player: Must bind on fully behind or alongside the hind-most team mate. Players cannot jump on top of the maul, drag others out of it, or intentionally bring it to ground. Such misdemeanours bring about a penalty. A free kick is awarded for trying to fool the other side into thinking the ball is out of the maul.

A successful end of a maul is when: The ball goes to ground or leaves the maul. A ball carrier can go to ground in a maul, but the ball must be immediately available to play.

What is a maul?
A maul occurs when a ball carrier is held by one or more opponents, and one or more of the ball carrier's team mates bind on to him. It consists of at least three players, all on their feet; the ball carrier and one player from each team. All the players must be caught in or bound to the maul, on their feet and moving towards a goal line.

Coach's notes

 What to call out
"Hips below shoulders"
"Chin off your chest"
"Bind with your full arm"

 What to look for
Players not balanced on entering the maul. They must stay on their feet, and keep the maul from collapsing.
Players offside at the maul.

 What to think about
Securing maul ball: keep it from defenders, stay on your feet, drive forward with short steps.
Stopping a maul: drive through the centre, hold onto the ball to prevent release.

The maul

Offside at the maul

OFFSIDE LINE

An unsuccessful end of a maul is when: A maul has stopped moving forward for more than 5 seconds. If the ball is available, the referee may allow some time for it to be released. Otherwise he orders a scrum. If a maul collapses, a scrum is awarded, unless because of foul play, in which case a penalty is awarded.

Whose scrum is it after a maul? The team not in possession of the ball when the maul started. If there is a doubt as to who had the ball, the referee gives the ball to the side that is going forward.

An exception is: A player who catches the ball from a kick other than a restart and then immediately becomes part of a maul. If a scrum is then awarded, the catcher's team will have the put-in.

Offside at the maul: The maul has an offside line on the back foot of the hindmost player. A player can only join by binding on or alongside this player. Any player not involved in the maul must retire behind the offside line.

Securing maul ball

The session

What you tell your players the session is about:

1 Retaining possession and going forward in a maul.
2 Committing defenders to create space elsewhere.
3 Working together and communicating in a maul.

What you tell your players to do:

1 The ball carrier should go into the contact on his feet, turned slightly, with the ball on one hip, and carried in one or two hands.
2 The second player into the contact should drive in and put his hands on the ball, so there are now three or four hands on the ball. The next player to arrive should drive in and work the ball towards himself.
3 A successful maul is due to the collective effort of all the players involved. Communicate to work together.

Securing maul ball

What you get your players to do:

Warm-up: Set up a 3 v 1 maul in a 5 metre square box. At walking pace, the three players have to move the maul from one corner to another without leaving the box.

Coach's notes

 What to call out

"Three or four hands on the ball until it can be moved back" (that is, two players drive in together, holding onto the ball)

"Take short driving steps, not walking"

"Keep low body positions"

"Ball carrier: tell the others who you are"

"Get the ball to the back"

 What to look for

Defenders getting their hands on the ball. Create a "seal" around the ball, by putting bodies between the defenders and the ball.

The maul slowing down or stopping. Look to change the axis of attack by rolling off in another direction.

Getting the ball trapped in the middle of the maul.

 What to think about

What is the role of the scrum half? Why should the backs practise mauling? How can you change a ruck into a maul? When should you use a maul in a game? What are the laws relating to the maul? When should the ball be released to the scrum half?

The maul

Practice: Set up a 5 metre box within a 15 metre square. Three players in the box pick up a ball and drive towards the side of the square. Three defenders in the square prevent this. They are not allowed in the box. The ball can only be transferred by a maul, with no passing. When you shout "CHANGE", the teams swap around.

Developing the session

The training session can be developed as follows.

1   Add an attacker and ensure at least one attacker is not attached to the maul.
2   Allow the defenders to tackle inside the smaller box and before the maul has formed, thus encouraging players to stay on their feet.
3   Allow the attackers three attempts, to "score", but move the "try line" each time.

A game situation

The session can be developed further by playing the following game. Split your players into two teams. On a narrow, long pitch (for instance, 10 metres wide and 50 metres long), place two balls 5 metres either side of the half way line. Each team is nominated a ball.

You shout the name of one of the teams. This team moves to their ball and one player picks it up. The other team forms a defensive line 2 metres away. When you blow the whistle the team with the ball attacks by mauling only. When the maul breaks down, for whatever reason, you blow the whistle and the teams have three seconds to reset. The other team now attacks with their own ball.

The driving maul

The session

What you tell your players the session is about:

1 Creating a driving maul with three players in an "arrowhead" and the ball carrier at the back.
2 Controlling a maul so the ball carrier can detach and attack.

What you tell your players to do:

1 Ball carrier: slow down before contact and turn to face your support.
2 Stay on your feet in contact.
3 The first support player must always secure the ball.
4 Create a "skin" of players around the ball and move it to the back of the maul.

5 Form the maul into an "arrowhead" or "dart" shape.
6 Scrum half: direct the drive and be aware of your options.

What you get your players to do:

Four players line up in a 7 metre channel, with one in front of another and two at each side. Facing a defender only a few metres away, the first player picks up a ball and drives into the defender. Staying on their feet, the other attackers bind on, with the second player ripping the ball. When the maul goes more than four metres (indicated by a line), the ball carrier breaks loose and then goes into the next contact. Repeat twice more along the channel.

Coach's notes

What to call out

"Talk the ball back"

"Three or four hands on the ball until it can be moved back" (that is, two players drive in together, holding onto the ball)

"Take short, sharp steps. Bend the knees"

"Ball carrier: keep the ball away from the opposition"

"Ball carrier: slow down – wait for support, don't get isolated"

"Don't let the opposition see the ball"

What to look for

The ball carrier getting into a poor position in contact. They must shield the ball from the opposition and open up their body enough for a support player to rip it clear.

The ball carrier taking contact without adequate support and so is forced to the ground or turned.

Binding players not protecting the ball carrier. They must get their hips at least in line with the front player and turn inwards to avoid opponents coming through the middle.

What to think about

When are mauls most likely to be used? What communication should be used, e.g. when to break? What are the likely actions of the opposition and how can these be countered?

The maul

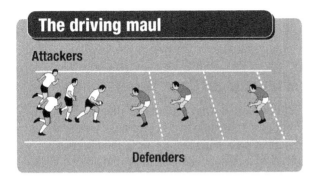

The driving maul

Attackers

Defenders

Developing the session

The training session can be developed as follows.

1 The defenders try to bring down the ball carrier before the maul is formed.
2 Have two defenders on each line.
3 Set a time limit to get to the end of the channel.
4 The attackers have to start outside the side edge of the box and run in, like from the side of a ruck.

A game situation

The session can be developed further by playing the "mauling gauntlet" game. Widen the channel to about 10 metres, with three lines about 10 metres apart. Set up two teams with equal numbers. Split the defence so that half of the defenders have to defend the middle line and the rest the last line. The attackers are thrown the ball and use any normal means possible to score. The defenders on the middle line can help the defenders on the last line, but not vice versa. Adjust the width of the channel so that when all the defenders are in a line, they cover the width at about an arm's distance apart.

Defending a maul

The session

What you tell your players the session is about:

1 Preventing the progress of an opponent's maul.
2 Safe and legal techniques to win the maul.
3 Making decisions about how best to defend against a maul.

What you tell your players to do:

1 Stop the maul before it starts.
2 Drive the maul backwards or sideways by PUSHING the maul from one side and PULLING it from the other.
3 Try to split up the maul.

What you get your players to do:

Practice 1: In a 5 metre box, have two players start at one end with a ball. The first player binds onto the second player. A defender, starting from the other

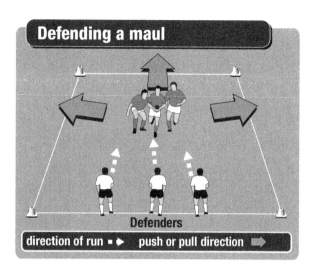

Defending a maul

Defenders

direction of run ▪ ▶   push or pull direction ⬛▶

end, walks forward and tries to tackle the ball carrier to the ground by grabbing them by the waist and pulling them down.

Practice 2: In the same box, set up two teams, one with three attackers, the other with three defenders.

Coach's notes

 What to call out

"First defender: tackle the ball carrier to the ground"

"Push and pull the maul to the nearest touchline" OR "Drive through the centre of the maul, not the sides" (it is not possible to do both – you can only drive through the centre of the maul if it is stationary)

"Take short sharp steps to gain momentum"

 What to look for

Players not making a contribution to preventing the maul moving forward. Players with a loose binding should leave the maul and rejoin through the back.

Players making poor decisions when defending. In the slow motion part of a drill get the players to "talk" through what they are trying to do as they do it.

 What to think about

The defender in the maul nearest the ball may be able to work their hands in to grab the ball. A slow, "feeling" action can be better than a "smash and grab". Can your players twist the maul? How many players do you want to commit to defending the maul? Do you need your backs to practise mauling?

The maul

The defenders need to drive the maul out of the box, using "stop the maul" techniques.

Start all the drills at walking pace, then progress in speed as the players become more adept.

Developing the session

The training session can be developed as follows.
1   Change the balance of play by adding defenders or attackers.
2   Change the starting distances between the teams (sometimes only half a metre, for example).

A game situation

The session can be developed further by playing the following "lineout" game.

Create some 4 v 4 (or more if you have the players) lineouts. Guarantee possession to one side. With senior players, start the game with them in the lifted position.

The attacking side has to score as if they are driving from a 5 metre lineout. If they are successful, they then move 3 metres further away and try again. Be vigilant on illegal attempts to stop the maul.

Ruck to maul

The session

What you tell your players the session is about:

1 Setting up a maul from a ruck.
2 Developing a static to a dynamic situation.

What you tell your players to do:

1 Communicate at a slow ruck that a maul is going to be set up, e.g. call "tiger ball".
2 Take the ball into contact in pairs. Player one works to stay on their feet. Player two targets the ball and drives.
3 Retain possession through the player furthest from the first point of contact.

What you get your players to do:

Practice 1: Set up a 2 v 1 with two attackers (A1 and A2) against one defender (D). A1 picks up the ball. A2 binds on and they drive into D. Ensure

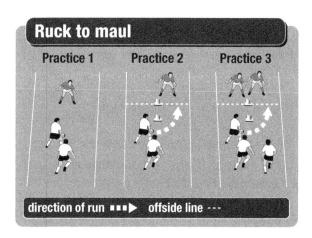

Ruck to maul

Practice 1   Practice 2   Practice 3

direction of run ■■■▶   offside line ---

both attackers have their hands on the ball into the contact.

Practice 2: Repeat practice 1, with players A1 and A2 going around a cone, representing the back feet of a ruck, before the contact.

Practice 3: Add another attacker and defender in the "post" positions, no more than two arms' lengths

Coach's notes

 What to call out

"Three or four hands on the ball before contact" (that is, two players drive in together, holding onto the ball)

"Drive forward from "low to high" – drive your opponent up on contact. Take short steps and pump the legs"

"Attack close to the ruck, don't go sideways. Look for space"

"Get the ball to the back of the maul"

 What to look for

Players isolated in contact. Ensure good communication and awareness between the players.

Players falling over. They need to keep a strong base in the contact, take short steps and keep a balanced body shape. The player should be "self-supported" – if the defender falls over, the player must still stay on their feet.

 What to think about

Where and when should you "ruck to maul"? How many players should you commit to a maul? Just forwards? How does a maul build with more than two players? How could players "roll" the maul? Drive and then roll outwards, away from the ruck? Should the "ruck to maul" then turn into another ruck? When do you want the ball delivered?

The maul

from their inside team mate. Their jobs are to attack or defend outside the ruck, or double up to attack or defend beside the ruck.

Developing the session

The training session can be developed as follows.

1. Set a time after which the ball must be released.
2. Ensure the defenders make decisions about the different ways to defend. For instance, tackling attackers to the ground (this isn't allowed once the maul has set), or trying to drive players back.
3. Award points for drives that go more than 3 metres, providing players remain on their feet.

A game situation

The session can be developed further by playing a small-sided game (e.g. 4 v 4) in a narrow area (e.g. a 10 metre square). The objective is to encourage players to stay on their feet in contact and maintain go forward momentum.

Set up two teams along opposite edges of the square. Place a ball near the attacking team. This team has to collect the ball off the ground and work as a unit to carry it over the defending team's line. The attackers must stay on their feet throughout.

The attacking team has three attempts to score. Any error results in a failed attempt. The defenders can also "steal" the ball or push the attackers out of the square. After three goes, swap the teams so the defenders become the attackers and vice versa.

The scrum

Scrum basics

The session

What you tell your players the session is about:

1 Understanding the basic body positions for the scrummage.
2 Understanding the basic foot positions for the scrummage.

What you tell your players to do:

1 Keep the hips below shoulders and the "spine in line".
2 Have a steady base across both feet, with the feet slightly wider than a shoulder width apart.

What you get your players to do:

Warm-up 1: One partner lies on their back, their body as straight and rigid as possible. The other partner rolls them along like a log.

Good body position

Coach's notes

 What to call out

"Push your chest through and shoulders up"
"Keep your knees under your hips"
"Keep your chin off your chest"
"Bend at the hips, not with your back"

 What to look for

The players' feet not set square. Use a line as a guide to help them build a mental picture and "muscle memory". Players not keeping the back parallel to the ground. Use the "angry cat/happy cat" demonstration. "Angry cat" has its back arched up, which is wrong. Make the players reverse this position for the ideal shape. Can you balance a ball on their back?

 What to think about

Revising this practice regularly during the season to maintain good technique.

The scrum

Scrum warm-up 4

Developing the session

The training session can be developed to improve player stance as follows.

Foot placement: A player pushes with two hands against some form of static resistance, for instance a wall, fence or even another player kneeling at right angles. Adjust the feet to make sure they are parallel.

Body shape: Starting with a player on all fours, adjust the chin, chest and back so that a ball can be balanced on their back. Get them to walk about with a ball balanced on their back and their head up.

Warm-up 2: One partner lies on their back, their body as straight and rigid as possible. The other partner tries to lift them up by the shoulders until they are standing. Keep the body straight and rigid.

Warm-up 3: "Plank push" – One partner stands. The other kneels in front of them and puts two hands on their chest to stop them falling forward. The kneeling player takes one hand away and holds for five seconds. They change hands and hold again. The standing partner should be in a leaning, straight position throughout.

Warm-up 4: Two players interlock arms, back to back. Then, in a controlled manner they rise up and down, keeping their chins of their chest.

The three man scrum

The session

What you tell your players the session is about:

1 Binding as a front row.
2 How the front row engages.

What you tell your players to do:

Bind tight enough so the hooker can strike whilst held secure. (Note: Don't hold the players in an engagement for more than 10 seconds.)

What you get your players to do:

Binding on the hooker

1 The hooker stands with his hands above his head.
2 The first player (who is going to be the left hand side loose-head or prop) puts his right hand on the right side of the hooker and then swings round into position.
3 The right hand or tight-head prop binds with the left hand to the right hand side of the hooker.

Loose-head binding on a hooker

Coach's notes

 What to call out

"Go left with the head"
"Look through the eyebrows"
"Bind tight, but don't grip tight"
"Keep hips and shoulders square"

 What to look for

Tired arms. Use the walk around bind.

Unstable scrums. Check the distances between the front rows. Are their hips and shoulders square? Are the players bending at the hip and knees before engagement?

 What to think about

Think about the bind being a quick and efficient process. Players must be comfortable with the system of binding and work easily with each other.

The props provide a stable platform for the hooker to support themselves. If the hooker is not comfortable, rethink the binding.

The scrum

The three man scrum

4   You shout the start of the engagement sequence "CROUCH, BIND" and then break.

Engaging against another three

1   Go through the binding sequence but with the players on their knees, finishing the engagement. Use the commands, "CROUCH, BIND, ENGAGE".
2   Check the players' bindings and then break.
3   Repeat the process at another place on the pitch.

Building the process

1   After the engagement and still on their knees, the front rows should rock back and forward gently.
2   Progress to practising this drill with the players standing.

The five man scrum

The session

What you tell your players the session is about:

1 Binding the locks.
2 How a competitive engagement works with hooking.

What you tell your players to do:

1 Bind together and then drive to win the put in.
2 Work together as a unit to maximise the full potential.

Binding around the waist

At junior levels, the locks should bind around the waist band of the props. Some international sides actually used the technique until quite recently.

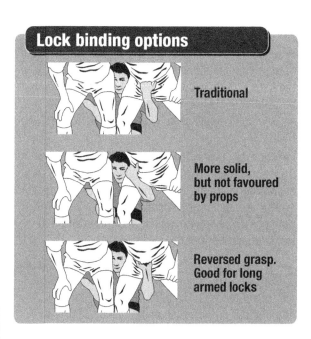

Lock binding options

Traditional

More solid, but not favoured by props

Reversed grasp. Good for long armed locks

Coach's notes

 ### What to call out

"Listen to the "triggers" (the binding calls)"

"Locks: generate force through the props – don't drive on the hooker"

"Take small steps and keep your knees bent"

"Make sure the hooker is comfortable"

 ### What to look for

When the two sides have engaged, the locks' shoulders should be just below the "shelf" of where the leg meets the buttock. The locks' shoulders need to start just below this point and then slide up on the engagement.

 ### What to think about

Binding through the legs:

a A lock can bind on the knot of the draw string of the prop's shorts. The players will find it easier if the prop guides the hand to the appropriate place.

b A stronger bind is on the pocket of the prop closest to the hooker. This pulls the arm into the leg.

The scrum

What you get your players to do:

Practice 1 – locks: Set up a 3 v 3 drill with two pairs of players each bound together. A lock binds onto the back of each group. Check the binding. Repeat, but this time the two sides gently engage. The engagement sequence at all levels is: "CROUCH, BIND, SET".

Practice 2 – locks: Set up a 5 v 5 drill with three front rowers and two locks. The locks bind on to each other and then on to the prop and hooker. You go through the engagement sequence, check for bindings and body positions, and then call break. Reset at another point.

Swap players around so they can experience different aspects of scrummage, BUT only as part of a slow, controlled process. Once the scrums become competitive, no player should be made to play in a position in which they don't feel comfortable.

Practice 3 – hooking: Set up a 3 v 2 scrum, where the hooking side have three players. An extra player can act as scrum half. He stands on the left hand side of the scrum. Get the two sets of players to fold in gently with the scrum engagement sequence. Then, on an agreed signal, the ball is put in down the centre of the tunnel and the hooker strikes for the ball. Depending on his style, he may either "drag kick" the ball back through the legs of his left hand prop or just let the momentum of ball deflect off the leg. Do not allow the players to push.

Developing the session

1 Add the other prop and allow a "striking" competition for the ball.
2 Allow one side or the other to push forward up to half a metre on the strike.
3 Add in all the other players.

Building a full scrum

The session

What you tell your players the session is about:

1 Binding together and building an eight man scrum. Remember to always follow the "CROUCH, BIND, SET" sequence.
2 Simple back row moves.

What you tell your players to do:

1 How the back row adds to the scrummage.
2 Simple tactics from the back row.

What you get your players to do:

Practice 1: Use a prop, a lock and a flanker against a scrum machine (or the prop can lean against a solid object). Check the binding and body positions.

Practice 2: Use a hooker, a prop and a lock against a prop, a lock and a flanker. Check the binding and body positions of the flanker.

1, 4 and 6 working together

Practice 3: Bind the players together in a circle. Practice the scrum engagement sequence. They should dip down together on the "CROUCH", squeeze together on the "SET" and then explode when you shout "BALL IN".

Coach's notes

 What to call out

"The flankers must scrummage first"
"Engage as an eight"
"The hooker must be comfortable"

 What to look for

Incorrect binding by the flankers. They must keep their full arm bound onto the lock forward.

 What to think about

Communication for the back row. Do they know what moves the backs are planning? Can they provide quick support? Where does the scrum half stand? How should the "8" hold the ball at the back of the scrum – right foot or left foot? Check your age grade laws for number "8" binding and when they can use back row moves.

The scrum

Practice 4: Bind the locks and the back row together and engage, without pressure, on the front row as opposition. The ball is passed through the scrum to the number eight who has to manipulate it for the scrum half to pass away. Repeat this process for back row moves.

Developing the session

The training can be developed using a scrum machine as follows.

1   Building the scrum. Put the elements together against a scrum machine. Ensure the hooker practises striking for the ball, using his heel or the side of the foot, and through the legs of the loose-head (left side) prop.

2   Practise individual technique. Go back to first principles: set square, backs straight, heads up, hips below shoulders, legs bent, front studs of boots only in the ground.

3   Practise front row binding and engagement, focusing on changing the heights the players engage.

4   Encourage aggression in the engagement and good body positions, as well as the timing of the front five and hooker.

5   Practise "unit" skills such as the one prop, a flanker and lock (1, 4, 6 or 3, 5, 7).

A game situation

The session can be developed with further practises against a scrum machine, particularly involving back row moves. For example, have the number 8 pick up and run right, before passing to the scrum half (the "9"). Or, have the scrum half run right, and pass back to the "8".

The lineout

Lineout jumping

The session

What you tell your players the session is about:

1 Reacting, jumping, catching and delivering the ball in one action.
2 Mastering the clean delivery of the ball to an awaiting player.

What you tell your players to do:

1 Keep the elbows in. Focus on your hands in the air.
2 Drive up with the legs, but relax the hands.
3 Deliver the ball "sympathetically" to another player.

What you get your players to do:

Set up a 10 metre square. One player, known as the "jumper" stands in the centre. Four other players stand in the middle of each side. One player starts with the ball, facing the jumper. The player counts down from three and throws the ball above the head of the jumper who has to catch and deliver it to the player standing on their right. This continues around the box until the ball reaches the first thrower. Repeat the practice anti-clockwise.

Leaping for the ball in the lineout

Coach's notes

 What to call out

"Look through your hands to catch the ball"

"Turn your hips to pass the ball to another player"

"Bend at the elbows when receiving the ball"

"Let the ball drop from the hands to the awaiting player"

 What to look for

The ball being tapped or slapped to the awaiting player. Players must control the ball by taking it and releasing it softly.

Not enough height from the jumper. Make sure they are leaping from a two foot, balanced stance, and bending at the knees.

 What to think about

Where should the hands be before the jump, at hip height or by the face? In what circumstances would you want your jumper to deliver the ball straightaway and when should it be gathered and held? It is important to jump and deliver without support (lifters).

The lineout

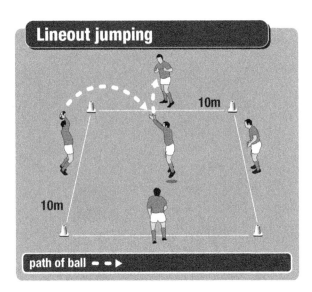

Lineout jumping

10m

10m

path of ball ➖ ➖ ▶

Developing the session

The training session can be developed as follows.

1 If your players are old enough, include lifters.

2 Adjust the distance of the throw. The ball should only be delivered from the jumper over a distance of 5 metres or less.

3 Have the players pass the ball around the square and throw it in when the jumper might not expect it.

4 Make the jumper leave the square after every jump, or perform an exercise to help him develop his concentration.

5 Award points for good leaps and delivery.

Lineout lifting

The session

What you tell your players the session is about:

1 Lifting the jumper and decoys in the lineout.
2 Quick, accurate and safe jumping and supporting.

What you tell your players to do:

1 The jumpers must initiate the jump.
2 The supporters drive the jumper up quickly and then hold him, before bringing him down safely.

What you get your players to do:

Set up two throwers and two "pods" of players (one jumper and two lifters or supporters). The pods face each other about 7 metres from their respective throwers. The first thrower throws into the first pod. This pod then passes the ball to the second pod, which throws the ball back to their thrower. The process is repeated in reverse, with the ball returning via both pods to the first thrower.

Successful lifting and jumping

Three key factors:

1. Body taut

2. Jumper goes straight up

3. Lifters close together

Coach's notes

 What to call out

"The jumper must jump first"
"Jumper: point your toes downwards"
"Lifters: bend your legs and arms"
"Lifters: step forward, at the end of the lift"

 What to look for

The jumper must not have their elbows back and close to their body before jump.

The jumper needs to jump using the hips, knees and ankles.

Players can replicate a weightlifter's clean and jerk.

What to think about

The lifters' grip. On the shorts allows for a good initial lift, but is not so good at the top of the lift. On the thigh can intially force the elbows out, but is better at the top of the lift, with the back lifter's hands acting as a seat for the jumper.

The lineout

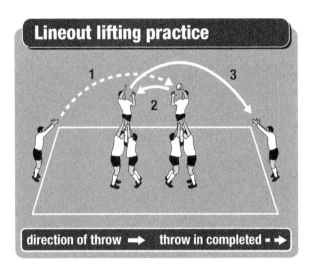

Lineout lifting practice

direction of throw ➡ throw in completed ▪▪➡

Developing the session

The session can be developed as follows. Set up one thrower and one pod (one jumper and two lifters). Lay out three cones as markers, 3 metres apart, with the thrower 5 metres away at another cone. Each cone is given a number (in the illustration 1, 2, 3). Call out two numbers. The pod moves quickly to the first cone called, performs a dummy jump and then moves to the second cone called, where they then jump for real.

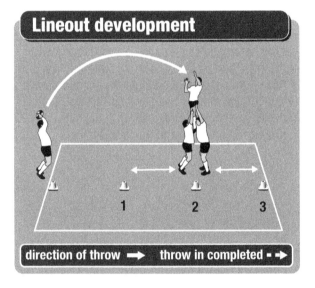

Lineout development

direction of throw ➡ throw in completed ▪▪➡

Lineout throw in

The session

What you tell your players the session is about:

1 Making accurate throw ins to the front, middle and back of the lineout.
2 Perfecting the different types of throw in.

What you tell your players to do:

1 Throw the ball for the jumper to meet at the top of their jump.
2 The whole body needs to move down the line of the throw.

What you get your players to do:

Set up a warm-up exercise with a jumper and a thrower, with the thrower on their knees. The thrower tries to hit the jumper at different distances. The jumper puts the hands down then up to indicate the top of the jump. Vary between flat (fast) throws and lobs (slow looped) throws.

Good hand positions for throwing

Coach's notes

 What to call out

"Keep both feet on the ground when throwing"

"Use the large muscles in the back and legs to start the throw"

"Complete the throw with the arms and hands using smaller muscles"

"Keep the elbow of the dominant hand tucked in"

 What to look for

The thrower unbalanced at the end of the throw. The body must not rotate around its axis. Instead the hips and shoulders should move forward.

Long throws falling short. The players should keep the body upright in the throw, using large muscle groups to get the ball moving.

 What to think about

The foot position. A thrower can have their feet in parallel, or one foot in front of the other, whatever they feel most comfortable with, as long as they don't rotate the hips. The hand position. Normally the players should use two hands, with the dominant hand nearer the back of the ball. One hand can be used if this is more comfortable.

The lineout

Lineout throw in

jump

jump

9m

6m

direction of throw in ⟶

Developing the session

The training session can be developed as follows. Set up five or six of the following practices to involve all your players. Arrange three cones. The first two 6 metres apart, the third a further 9 metres back. The thrower stands by the first cone.

1 The jumper jumps first from a standing position at the second cone, then from in between the second and third cones, and then at the back cone. The ball is thrown for him to catch in the air with each jump.

2 The jumper starts by the 6 metre cone again. When the thrower pulls the ball back behind his head, the jumper walks backwards for a count of three seconds, stops and jumps. The thrower times the throw to hit the jumper.

3 As "2" above, but this time the jumper moves backwards from the six metre cone to the 15 metre cone, stops for three seconds and then jumps.

4 Repeat with the jumper walking forwards for three seconds and jumping at the 6 metre cone, and finally, running forwards to take a flat throw at the front cone.

Lineout catch and drive

The session

What you tell your players the session is about:

1 Catching the ball from the lineout and forming a maul.
2 Driving the maul forward.

What you tell your players to do:

1 The player catching the ball at the lineout (the "catcher") turns towards his team mates and presents the ball away from his body and to the "ripper".
2 Two players support the catcher by binding on to him to form a wedge (these would probably be the lifters in senior rugby).
3 The "ripper" takes the ball off the catcher and drives in on the catcher with the ball on the hip.
4 A fourth player binds onto the "ripper", before taking the ball and placing it on their hip.

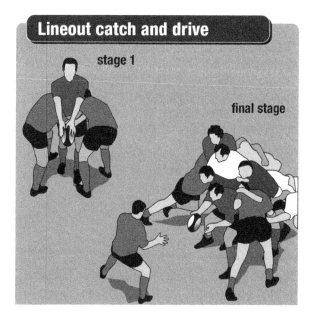

Lineout catch and drive

stage 1

final stage

5 The whole group then drives forward. Other players may support the maul by binding in at the back.

Coach's notes

 ### What to call out

"Catcher: pull in your supporters"

"First line of the maul: form into an arrow shape and drive forward"

"Ripper: pull the ball away before binding"

"Take short steps in the maul. You control the momentum"

 ### What to look for

Opposition players being able to get between the catcher and supporters. The supporters need to form a "skin" around the catcher, with a tight bind.

Players not driving forward from the initial catch. The drive does not need to be immediate. The ball must be secured first.

Once secured, however, the maul needs to drive forward without delay.

 ### What to think about

What happens once the ball has been secured and driven forward? Should the players "roll off" the side of the maul and attack the edges? Should the ball be moved to the back line? How many players do you want to commit to the maul? Who should play the role of the "ripper"? For example, the hooker at the front of the line, the player in the number 1 position in the lineout or a player in the middle of the lineout?

The lineout

What you get your players to do:

The catcher starts with the ball in his hands. He can either jump or be lifted, but when he returns to the ground the two players either side of him (who might be the supporters in the lift) bind on to his shorts and form a wedge. The next player in is designated the "ripper" and the maul is set up.

Initially, walk through the practice with different players taking on the various roles, and add players to create a full lineout set up.

Developing the session

The training session can be developed as follows.

1   Use a proper throw in, with the ball being caught and driven from the front or the middle of the lineout.
2   Include opposition players to compete for the throw and disrupt the lineout.

A game situation

The session can be developed further by playing the following game. Line up two equal sets of forwards on the 5m line. The attacking team has to win the lineout, form a maul and score over the try line. The defending team may win the lineout ball, disrupt the lineout and maul, hold up the maul, and otherwise find ways to prevent the try.

Match tactics

131 **Attacking channels**

Identifying the channel through which to launch a counter attack.
Getting the ball and support players into the least defended channel.

133 **Second phase ball**

Setting up quick second phase ball from the back of a scrum.
Support players making quick decisions to make quick ball.

135 **Converting opportunities**

Building pressure on opponents by going forward and retaining possession.
Converting opportunities near to the opponent's try line – the "red zone".

Attacking channels

The session

What you tell your players the session is about:

1 Identifying the channel through which to launch a counter attack.
2 Getting the ball and support players into the least defended channel.

What you tell your players to do:

1 The first player to the ball must secure it and then listen and observe.
2 Move the ball away from the initial catch or gather quickly.
3 Support players communicate where the space is.
4 The first supporter must move towards the ball carrier to offer options. Other players must move to likely reception points, i.e. spread themselves across the channels.

Attacking channels

Coach

A   B   C

direction of throw or kick ➡

What you get your players to do:

Set out three channels (A, B and C), with the middle channel wider than the others. Have a player stand in each channel, then throw or kick a ball into one of the channels. The player gathers the ball.

Coach's notes

💬 What to call out

"Ball carrier: pass and support"
"Supporters: tell the ball carrier where the space is"
"Ball carrier: move the ball away from the bulk of the defence"
"Ball carrier: move forward to get your supporters onside"

🔍 What to look for

Support players not running straight back. They should look to give the ball carrier options across the field.
The ball carrier running sideways. They should pass the ball, or look to switch the play. Running sideways gives up ground and makes it more difficult for the supporters to get onside.

💡 What to think about

Should the first player pass or switch to start a counter attack? When should the players kick? Where on the pitch should counter attacks start? Where should the support players aim to run to give themselves the best chance of getting back into the game?

Match tactics

All three players then move the ball, using switches, passes and loops, into another channel as designated by you. The players should try to finish in this channel by the time the ball carrier has passed you.

Developing the session

The training session can be developed as follows.

1 Add defenders to the channels. You should tell them which channel to move into. Then the attackers have to avoid the defenders when trying to move the ball to the designated channel. For example, set up the defenders in channel B, attackers in channel A, and throw the ball into channel C.

2 Vary the length and height of your throw or kick. Players might have to chase back, or take the ball when a defender is close.

A game situation

The session can be developed further by playing the "counter channels" game. Using the whole pitch, split your players into six counter attackers (CAs) and four defenders. Three CAs and two defenders stand by the coach. Two other defenders stand out like a backline whilst the other CAs are positioned in the back field. The coach kicks the ball and the play develops.

The aim is for the CAs to get level with the coach. With enough players, the kicker should be a player and he can have a pre-planned kick, worked out with his defenders. This way the CAs team has to choose carefully where to put its backfield players.

Second phase ball

The session

What you tell your players the session is about:

1 Setting up quick second phase ball from the back of a scrum.
2 Support players making quick decisions to make quick ball.

What you tell your players to do:

1 Attack close to the scrum aggressively to cross the gain line.
2 Support players provide the ball for the scrum half in space.

What you get your players to do:

Use four cones to represent the "feet" of the two locks at a scrum. Set two players on bended knee

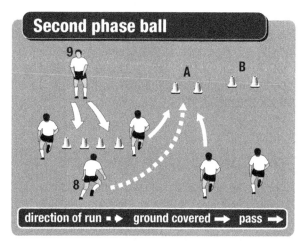

Second phase ball

direction of run ▪▶   ground covered ➡   pass ➡

either side of the cones, a number 8, with two backs standing further away. Place two pairs of cones forward from the "feet" cones. The first pair 5 metres forward and 5 metres to the right (as channel "A"), the second pair a further 2 metres forward and 2 metres to the right (channel "B").

Coach's notes

 ### What to call out

"Ball carrier: run low and hard. Take short powerful steps into the contact"

"Ball carrier: stay on your feet and drive your legs until support arrives"

"Supporters: communicate with the ball carrier – tell them when to go to ground"

"Get the ball clear of the contact as soon as possible"

 ### What to look for

The ball carrier getting isolated or falling over too quickly. They need to turn slightly towards the support players before contact.

Supporters over-running the ball carrier. They will not be in a position to protect the ball from the opposition. They need to keep back to see what is happening in front of them.

Attacking players not aligning deep enough to attack from the next phase.

 ### What to think about

Which way should the ball carrier turn? What are the benefits of turning in or turning out for each type of player? Does a mini maul or mini ruck suit your team? Are there circumstances where you can go left off the back of the scrum? What do you do next once you have recycled the ball quickly? Go wide, go back the other way – which would suit you? What other options can you use to commit defenders and create space?

Match tactics

A scrum half rolls the ball through the "feet" cones. The "8" picks up, and goes through channel A. The "8" then goes to ground or stays on his feet. The nearest two players secure the ball. The scrum half then passes the ball for the backs to attack channel B.

Developing the session

The training session can be developed as follows.

1 Add defenders into the channels. If you have ruck bags, then use these to start with.
2 Swap the players acting as backs into positions in the pack.
3 Change the position of channel "B". For example wider or on the other side of the "scrum".
4 Use any player as the scrum half and number "8".

A game situation

The session can be developed further by playing the "behind the 8 ball" game. Divide your players into two teams. Keep potential "8s" and "9s" in their positions if possible. Pack down a strictly unopposed scrum with equal numbers. Then use a back row move where the number "8" runs right. See if that team can create "quick ball".

The attackers have two tasks: create "quick ball" within three seconds of contact, and break the gain line. The defence has to try to stop both. Change the balance of players in the two teams depending on the success.

Converting opportunities

The session

What you tell your players the session is about:

1 Building pressure on opponents by going forward and retaining possession.
2 Converting opportunities near to the opponent's try line – the "red zone".

What you tell your players to do:

1 Balance the risks and be patient. Scoring opportunities will come.
2 Take territory in small stages, don't let up the pressure.
3 Support each other. Never take contact if there is no support.

What you get your players to do:

Set up two 20 metre square boxes joined together along one side. A group of players move around in

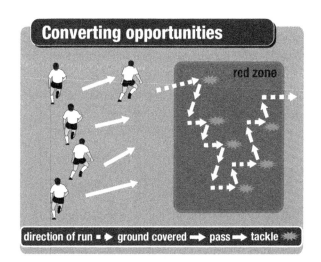

Converting opportunities

red zone

direction of run ▪▶ ground covered ➡ pass ➡ tackle ☀

any direction in one box, passing between each other. When the coach shouts "RED ZONE", the ball carrier runs into the next box. He then moves forward about 2 metres (adjust this distance accordingly) before either going to ground or turning for support.

Coach's notes

 What to call out

"Communicate where the gaps are"

"Always go forward, but keep the ball"

"Make flat passes close to the line"

"Make shorter passes closer to the line"

"Keep your depth in attack (runners coming from deep are harder to stop)"

 What to look for

Players getting close to the line and then throwing a long pass back too far which loses ground.

Players passing the ball to a static, upright player who loses ground or gets turned over in the tackle. Players must maintain low body positions close to line.

 What to think about

What might be the best backs moves to use? What is the role of the scrum half? What is the maximum number of passes your side can perform under pressure? Do you want to use rucks and mauls with your team? How can you most effectively suck in defenders to make space for your runners? At what stage do you want to give the ball to the backs in the "red zone"? For senior sides, how might "squeeze ball" be used?

Match tactics

The first supporter reacts by driving over, or driving in, and the ball is presented to a second supporter. It is then passed out, either one or two passes. The ball is again carried forward two metres.

Ideally this happens seven to eight times before the ball is passed to a player who scores. Shout "TACKLE" every time the two metres is gained.

Developing the session

The training session can be developed as follows.

1   You act as the line of defence, touching the ball carrier who goes to ground.
2   Dictate whether the ball from the breakdown is fast or slow. The players have to decide how to proceed.
3   Add defenders and eventually tackling.

A game situation

The session can be developed by playing a game of touch rugby where one team keeps hold of the ball until it is knocked forward or a forward pass is used. When touched, the ball carrier goes to ground immediately and the ball is passed away from the ground. Alternatively the player can remain on their feet and the next player rips the ball and passes. Develop with holding tackles, and then full contact. The defence is not allowed to compete for the ball when it is on the ground.

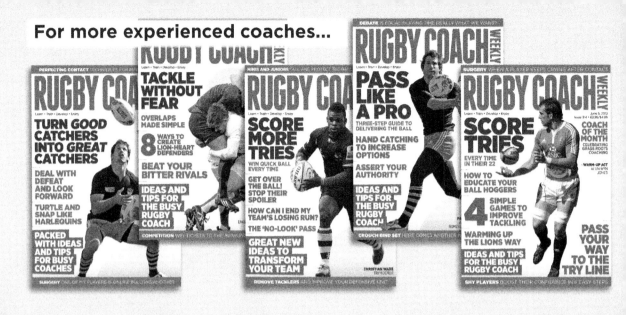

About the author

Dan Cottrell

Dan has spent most of his adult life collecting and absorbing the most useful rugby coaching secrets he can find. He is a practising RFU Level 3 Coach, a Welsh Rugby Union Course Leader, head coach for Swansea Schools U15s and a Level 2 referee. Dan played first class rugby at Bath and Bristol and later became Director of Rugby at Cranleigh School in Surrey.

Dan is best known as the editor of the successful free rugby coaching email *Better Rugby Coaching*, which has been published since 2003 and has 80,000 subscribers worldwide – www.betterrugbycoaching.com.

About Rugby Coach Weekly

Rugby Coach Weekly is an e-magazine that delivers quality rugby coaching activities and advice direct to your email inbox every week.

The team at *Rugby Coach Weekly* understands that coaching rugby is a big responsibility. Their aim is to make it easier and more fun for you. They recognise that as a coach, you're not just teaching people how to play a great sport, you're also giving them life skills such as self-confidence, teamwork and mental toughness.

That is why each issue of *Rugby Coach Weekly* is packed with expert advice tailored specifically for you as a new or grassroots coach, so you can be confident that you have exactly the right information to pass on to your team.

That advice comes in the shape of comprehensive coaching sessions so you always have an exciting, fresh coaching plan, containing training secrets from experienced professional coaches, at your finger tips. You will also find the latest news about law changes and coaching developments to keep you ahead of the game.

Rugby Coach Weekly aims to set new standards of excellence in rugby coaching. It will save you time, effort and aggravation every week, enrich your coaching experience and help you develop as a coach.

Lightning Source UK Ltd.
Milton Keynes UK
UKOW05f1958031117
312116UK00005B/511/P